*Advance Praise for*

# PENNSYLVANIA
## *Curiosities*

"From the story of our world-famous groundhog to the history of hoagies, *Pennsylvania Curiosities* covers it all with wit and charm. A delightful read for every Pennsylvanian with a sense of humor."

—Denise Remillard, Associate Publisher,
*Central Pennsylvania Parent*

"Pack your bags and get ready as DeLeon takes you on a hilariously informative trip around the Keystone State!"

—Anissa Rupert, Editor, *Where & When:
Pennsylvania's Travel Guide*

"*Pennsylvania Curiosities* is a great offbeat primer on Pennsylvania and its residents. Even lifelong Pennsylvanians can learn colorful history about the state they call home."

—Connie McNamara, Travel Editor, *Patriot-News*

*Curiosities Series*

# PENNSYLVANIA
## *Curiosities*

### QUIRKY CHARACTERS, ROADSIDE ODDITIES & OTHER OFFBEAT STUFF

*Clark DeLeon*

The Globe Pequot Press

Guilford, Connecticut

*To Eleanor,*

*because wings are a terrible
thing to waste*

All photos are by Clark DeLeon unless otherwise indicated
Cover design: Nancy Freeborn
Text design: Bill Brown
Cover photos: Clark DeLeon
Maps: Lisa Reneson

**Library of Congress Cataloging-in-Publication Data**
CIP is available.
0-7627-0892-1

Manufactured in the United States of America
First Edtion/Third Printing

# ACKNOWLEDGMENTS

I'd like to thank a number of people for their help in producing this book. First my thanks to Laura Strom of The Globe Pequot Press for approaching me with the idea of writing *Pennsylvania Curiosities* and for guiding it through to its completion. Thanks also to Mimi Egan, a former Pennsylvanian who was the project editor on the book, and to Karen Elliott for her skillfull copyediting.

I thank the late Jason Miller—actor, playwright, and friend—for his talent and for opening his home and his hometown of Scranton to me. I thank Casey Rhoades for the vast moment of silence we shared on the summit of Tuscarora Mountain on our way to Pittsburgh. Special thanks to Ted McKnight and his wife, Barbara, for their hospitality when my daughter Molly and I stayed in their clock-filled home in Lock Haven (once you get used to a half-dozen antique clocks chiming every quarter hour, it's almost as peaceful as the sound of crickets). Thanks of a different sort to L. A. "Larry" Rotheraine, a big city boy gone country, who is working on behalf of the angels in Lewis Run, Pennsylvania. Thanks of the usual "I am not worthy" sort to my wife of thirty years and my sweetheart forever, Sara.

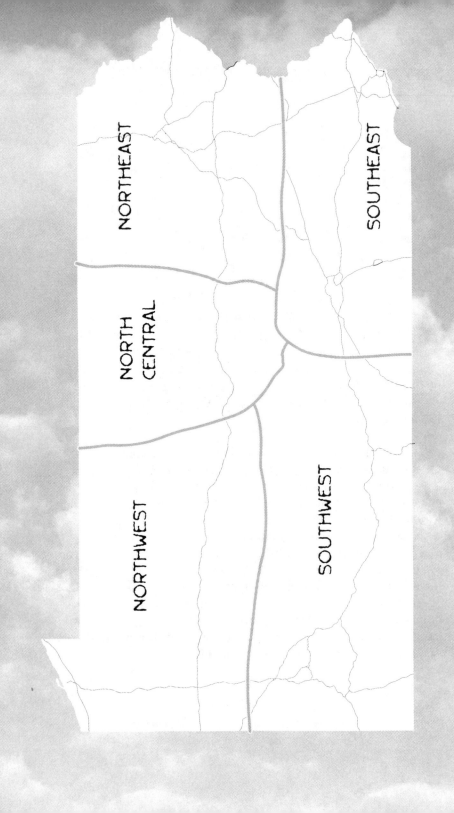

# Contents

Introduction
ix

Do Pennsylvanians Tawk Funny?
xi

Southeastern Pennsylvania
1

Southwestern Pennsylvania
97

Northeastern Pennsylvania
133

North Central Pennsylvania
163

Northwestern Pennsylvania
173

Index
203

*Many Pennsylvania towns were originally named after taverns.*

# INTRODUCTION

**M**ost Pennsylvanians know that Pennsylvania is the Keystone State. Considerably fewer Pennsylvanians know what a keystone is, and fewer still can explain why Pennsylvania is one. What Pennsylvanians don't know about Pennsylvania could fill a book. Not this book, but some book.

This book is about Pennsylvania curiosities. By definition, that means anything curious, strange, rare, or novel. But one person's curiosity might be another person's brother-in-law. What is strange, rare, or novel to you might be commonplace to the people who live next to Three Mile Island. What Pittsburgh calls an incline is that curious "thingy that goes up the side of the mountain" to someone from Philadelphia. What people in Bradford have to go around in the drive-through line at McDonald's is a working oil well, which are as common in McKean County as traffic lights in other parts of the state, but rather curious to those unaccustomed to ordering 10W-30 with their burgers.

My approach in writing this book was to look for things in and about Pennsylvania that I found curious—people, places, or stories that struck me as interesting. Especially things I didn't know before. Like most Pennsylvanians, I was born in Pennsylvania and have lived here my entire life. My parents, my grandparents, and my children were all born in Pennsylvania. I've worked as a newspaper columnist in Philadelphia for more than twenty-five years. You'd think I'd know a thing or two about Pennsylvania, and I thought I did, too, before I started researching this book. What I've learned in the process is how much I didn't know about my home state and how much more there is to know. I learned that Altoona is a Cherokee word meaning "highlands of great worth" and that Pennsylvania's only President of the United States was probably gay. Being from Philadelphia, I knew there was a typo on the Liberty Bell (Pennsylvania is spelled wrong), but I didn't know that Pittsburgh has been spelled Pittsburgh ever since its founding in 1758 except for a twenty-one-year period between 1890 and 1911 when the United States Board on Geographic Names decided Pittsburgh should be spelled Pittsburg. I learned that Heinz ketchup poured from the bottle travels at an average speed of 23 miles per year.

And then there was the traveling. Pennsylvania is a lot bigger in person, believe me. I had no idea that there were so many runaway truck ramps in Pennsylvania, but then, I didn't know there were so many mountains, either. I'm not going to say I put a lot of miles on my car, but I will say I know the names of the children of every toll taker on the Pennsylvania Turnpike. Along the way I visited a town in Crawford County where the ducks walk on the fish, and a city in York County that was the only northern city occupied by the Confederate Army during the Civil War. I saw the world's second-largest collection of Edsels and a town that's been on fire for more than thirty years. I saw a flying saucer in Mars and a famous groundhog in Punxutawney. I saw a herd of buffalo outside of Erie and the bottom of a coal mine outside of Scranton. I saw the mysterious handprint on the prison wall in Carbon County and the tomb of Jim Thorpe in the town that bears his name. I met people, asked questions, and heard stories. I discovered that what I didn't know about Pennsylvania could fill a book. This one.

# DO PENNSYLVANIANS TAWK FUNNY?

P ennsylvania is a lot like England and America, which Winston Churchill once described as "a great people divided by a common language." Yes, all or at least most Pennsylvanians speak English. But Pittsburgh speaks English its way, Scranton its way, Philadelphia its way, and, well, there's a reason that the Pennsylvania Dutch aren't called Pennsylvania English. *New York Times* "language" columnist William Safire noted the differences between spoken Pennsylvanian and spoken English when in 1983 he wrote about a friend who "roots for a football team he calls the Iggles [and] talks in a patois so incomprehensible" that he asked for help in understanding "words and pronunciations peculiar to people from Philadelphia." Because I grew up in Philadelphia, I am more familiar with the "patois" Mr. Safire spoke of, although real Philadelphians don't use words like *patois*.

To speak proper Philadelphian, it helps to understand the following terms:

*FLUFFYA: Ciddy of Brotherly Love*

*SENDA CIDDY: downtown Fluffya*

*KWAWFEE: what you buy at Dunkin' Donuts*

*WOODER: clear liquid that turns brown in kwawfee*

*WINDA: glass rectangle on the side of a house*

*WINDIZ: more than one winda*

*SHTREET: asphalt path used by cars.*

*PAYMENT: concrete path used by people*

*CROWNS: those little wax sticks you get in Crayola boxes*

*KELLER: crowns come in different kellers*

*ACKAMEE: big supermarket*

*INKWIRE: Fluffya's morning newspaper*

*PIXTURE: painting or photo hanging on the wall*

*PURDY: good looking, as in "purdy as a pixture"*

*CHIMBLY: hole in the roof that lets the smoke out*

*YOUSE: second person singular, "Youse lookin' at me?"*

*YIZZ: plural of youse*

*YIZZLE: contraction of youse will, as in "Yizzle be comin' over tonight, won'tchizz?"*

*VETCH-T-BLS: t'maydahs and p'taydahs*

*BUDDER: something to put on p'taydahs or a samitch*

*WUNST: half of twiced*

*STRAWBIDJEZ: a department store*

*FIFF: shtreet between Forf and Sixt, also called Fiss Shtreet*

*AKKROST: something you have to do to Fiff to get from Forf to Sixt Shtreet*

*AWN: opposite of awf*

*DINT: a denial, as in "I dint do it"; Sometimes pronounced "ditt'n"*

*WOOTNA: would not have, "Hey, even if I cooda, I wootna done it."*

*SUMP'N: not nothin'*

*POCK A BOOK: what a man wouldn't be caught dead carrying*

*TAL: cloth used to dry off after a shower*

*AST: to inquire in the past tense, as in, "I ast Gloria for a date, and she tole me to go take a wawk."*

*WIDGES: in your company, as in, "Hey, I'll go widges!"*

*HON: variation on Sir, Ma'am, or Miss as practiced in Philadelphia eating establishments, as in, "Yo, Hon, watches want with that hamburger?"*

*DOUNNASHORE: a summer destination, a place to swim and gamble, a.k.a. Lannick Ciddy*

*GAWNA: to depart or proceed to, as in, "And to think I was gawna taker dounnashore."*

*SKOOK'LE: river with a name that's really hard to spell*

*ADDYTOOD: what Fluffyans are proud to have*

Once you've mastered Philadelphian, Pittsburghese makes a lot more sense:

*PIXBURG: Pennsylvania's second largest ciddy*

*YUNZ: same as youse*

*WE UNZ: first person plural*

*YINZER: a Pixburg native, a person who says yunz and we unz*

*DAHNTAHN: senda ciddy Pixburg, also pronounced "dawn tawn"*

*DA BUCOS: National League baseball team sometimes called da Parrots*

*DA STILLERS: once great football team; two or more moonshiners*

*BLAST FURNACE: sound of the stadium when da Stillers win*

*GIANT IGGLE: local supermarket chain; what Fluffya's football team became during the 2000 NFL season*

*STEEGLES: name of Pennsylvania's football franchise during World War II when the Pixburg Stillers merged with the Fluffya Iggles*

*DA PENS: National Hockey League franchise in Pixburg*

*DA IGLOO: where da Pens play*

*FARCE FAR: what Smokey da Bear says only yunz can prevent*

*IT'S A BURG THANG: Pixburg expression Fluffyans wouldn't understand*

*SLIPPY: what roads get when wet*

*AHT: opposite of in*

*SLIBERTY: suburb of East Liberty*

*SAHSIDE: south side of the Monongahela River*

*STILL MILLS: what Pixburg used to have a lot of, why it was called "The Still Ciddy"*

*JUMBO: a big baloney sangwich, a Pixburg hoagie*

*QUIT JAGGIN DAT JUMBO: stop playing with your food*

*POND: what sixteen ounces equal*

*DAWN: a masculine name, short for Dawnald*

*RAW KNEE: a feminine name; also Scottish for pretty, as in a "baw knee lass"*

*EYE SEE LITE: a cold bottle of beer*

*POP: Coke, Pepsi, etc.*

*SPUTZIE: a noisy little bird*

*RADIO TOWER: steel-belted rubber around a wheel, cars use four at time*

*IMP n ARN: a shot and a beer, Imperial and Iron Ciddy*

*GUM BANDS: what rubber bands are called in Pixburg*

*MOUNT WARSHINGTON: big hill overlooking dahntahn*

With a working knowledge of the dialects in Pennsylvania's largest cities on the state's southeastern and southwestern extremities, understanding Northeast and Central Pennsylvania should be a piece of cake. But not necessarily. "Hayna," for instance, is an expression everyone up and down the line from Wilkes-Barre to Scranton uses or understands, but I have yet to meet someone who can explain it. "Hayna, you know, it means 'you know what I mean?'" an Old Forge resident told me. "Hayna or no." Make sense? OK, then you should have no problems with understanding North Central Pennsylvania-speak:

*HAYNA VALLEY: where people who say "hayna" live*

*WIXBERRY: what Scrantonyans call Wilkes-Barre*

*GIMME A STEG: I'll have a cold beer, please*

*MELK: white liquid kids drink before they're old enough for a Steg*

*PIGGIES: cabbage rolls that can be eaten with melk or beer*

*HALUSHKI: cabbage again, sautéed with pasta*

*DA YOU: the University of Scranton*

*DEE ACKAMEE: same as in Fluffya, "Meet me at dee Ackamee."*

*MAYAN: ancient Mexican civilization, also "that belongs to me"*

*LECKTRIC: Scranton is called the Lecktric City*

*BREFISS: first meal of the day*

*BAFF ROOM: where you go after eating brefiss*

*DRAFF: beer served cold from the tap*

*LIE BERRY: classy place with books*

The Pennsylvania Dutch have added their own flavor to the Pennsylvania language stew. How else do you think Kutztown High School could come up with a cheer that goes, "Ring baloney once! Ring baloney twice! Hey, yah, Kutztown sure is nice!"

*GETT'N TO WET'N: looks like rain*

*LEP'NEN: county adjoining Lancaster; a type of baloney*

*STOP BEING SO SHUSSLY: can't you walk without tripping over your own feet?*

*OUTEN THE LIGHTS: don't waste electricity*

*THE BABY'S GREXY: my, what a cranky baby*

*WOOTZ: a person who makes a pig of himself at dinner*

*RAISON STROP: Amish buggies don't have them painted on the sides, but hot rods do*

*FRESSING: indulging a sweet tooth, a wootz with candy*

*HURRIEDER: what you can't do in traffic stuck behind an Amish buggy*

*MISHTY: nickname for an Amish person*

*DIPPY X: flip those eggs over easy*

*CROTCH: enclosed place to park the car*

*THROW MAMMA FROM THE CAR A KISS: kiss me from the window*

*QUIT YER BRUTZIN: you're acting like a grexy*

*COME THE HOUSE IN: but first off the wipe feet*

*TASTES LIKE MORE: are you serving seconds?*

SOUTHEAST

# SOUTHEAST

## THE BLAND TRUTH
### Bala Cynwyd

James Bland, the African-American composer who wrote "Carry Me Back to Old Virginny," is buried in West Laurel Hill Cemetery in a Montgomery County town with a Welsh name, Bala Cynwyd. Among the ironies of Bland's life and legacy is the fact that he was the author of the Mummers' anthem, "Oh, Dem Golden Slippers." Although when he died penniless in Philadelphia in 1911, and for decades after his death, Bland would not have been welcomed as a member in most Mummer clubs in the city where he lived his last years. During his musical career, he was celebrated in Europe as a composer and performer, but when he returned to the United States he couldn't get work in minstrel shows because only white men in blackface were hired to portray black men.

For the record, here are the words to the chorus or refrain of "Golden Slippers," written by Bland in 1879:

*Oh, dem golden slippers!*
*Oh, dem golden slippers!*
*Golden slippers I'se gwine to wear,*
*Bekase dey look so neat.*
*Oh, dem golden slippers!*
*Oh, dem golden slippers!*
*Golden slippers I'se gwine to wear,*
*To walk de golden street.*

## DANIEL BOONE WAS A PENNSYLVANIA KIND OF GUY
### Birdsboro

"**D**aniel Boone was a man. Yes, a real man." So goes the theme song to the old *Daniel Boone* TV show starring Davy Crockett (or was it Fess Parker?). Daniel Boone was also a Quaker, or at least he started life that way. Boone was born in 1734 in a log cabin in Berks County in what is now called Birdsboro. There is a stone farmhouse where his log birthplace once stood, but the original earth-floored cellar and spring remain from the structure that Boone called home for the first sixteen years of his life. That was about as long as the frontiersman ever stayed in one place, because from the time he turned twenty-one until his death at the age of eighty-five in Missouri in 1820, Daniel Boone was a man on the move.

The Daniel Boone Homestead off Route 422 is a collection of eighteenth century buildings maintained and operated by the Pennsylvania Historical and Museum Commission. You can learn about Boone's travels in a twelve-minute video in the visitor center. ("Them Boones was always lookin' for more elbow room, if you know what I mean," says the colonially dressed narrator of the documentary.) Daniel was the sixth of eleven children born to Squire Boone and his wife, Sarah. The Boones were Quakers from Devonshire, England, who had come to Pennsylvania seeking the religious freedom and opportunities promised by the commonwealth's proprietor, William Penn.

Young Daniel was a gun-toting Quaker. He became a proficient shot with a long gun that would become famous as the Pennsylvania rifle when he moved to Kentucky in later life. After Squire Boone had a falling out with his fellow Quakers over the issue of one of his children marrying a non-Quaker, the family began a trek southward and westward that would take them to through Maryland and Virginia and finally to North Carolina, where they settled when Daniel was sixteen. At the age of twenty-one, Daniel married Rebecca Byrne, a woman who would spend most of her life wondering where that husband of hers had gotten himself this time—either being captured by Indians or leading a raiding party or exploring new territory and settling communities named in his honor, such as Boonesborough, Kentucky. Daniel was home enough to leave Rebecca with ten children, however.

Daniel Boone's Pennsylvania years were the stuff of storybooks, which means you could make up stories about them because so little is known about his youth. He did return to his birthplace twice, in 1781 and 1788, to visit relatives who had purchased the homestead from his father. Today the homestead is as much about the settlers who carved out a life in the sparsely populated wilderness of central Pennsylvania. There is a flintlock rifle range where specialty competitions are held on the 579-acre property that the state took over in 1938. There are a total of seven structures on the site, including a restoration of the original eighteenth century smokehouse, blacksmith shop, and sawmill.

The Daniel Boone Homestead, on Daniel Boone Road in Birdsboro, is open year-round. Call (610) 582–4900.

## BUCKS COUNTY CHAIN SAW ARTIST
### Buckingham

When I first spotted Larry Homan, he was sitting in a chair atop a pile of wood chips behind what looked like a cigar store Indian and a grizzly bear just off the side of the road on Route 202 in Buckingham, Bucks County. Curious, I thought. Behind him were a pile of tree trunks and thick

*Crouching tiger, hidden chainsaw. Tree stump sculptor Larry Homan works on another creature.*

stumpy cross sections of trees with the bark still on them. In the middle of it all was a work in progress, a large feline head beginning to emerge from a hunk of wood about four feet wide and three feet high. "It'll be a tiger when it's done," Homan tells me, pointing to a schematic drawing of a crouching tiger in a sketch book. And then he got to work with his chain saw.

Homan operates a tree service business ("tree pruning, tree removal, acreage cleared"), and about a year and a half ago he began to explore ways to make the wretched refuse of his daily labor into something else entirely. Animals mostly, lions and tigers and bears, oh my, parrots and owls and horse heads. "I'm not an artist," he says, shaping the tiger with one of the three sizes of chain saws he uses on most pieces. "I just like animals."

It takes two to four hours to complete a piece, depending on the size and whether it is painted or varnished. He works on his figures during downtime between jobs or at the end of the day. His chain saw art sells in the $200 to $600 range, and he gets his fair share of drive-up business. "It's not something you can buy at K-mart," he says, pointing to a bear cub flowerpot. Homan is modest about the unique nature of his side business. "Ah, you'll see chainsaw sculpture every 150 miles or so," he says. I must report that I've put several thousand miles on my car driving around Pennsylvania since I saw Homan, and I haven't seen another one yet.

## MASHED POTATO MURDERESS MEETS SERIAL BREAD SQUEEZER
### Bucks County

Bucks County Court Judge David Heckler had heard his share of odd cases during his three years on the bench. There was the lady who waved a gun at passing skateboarders and there was the case in which he had to determine how far trailer homes should be parked from each other. But he could remain on the bench another twenty years without having the bizarre one-two of consecutive trials that greeted him in September 2000.

No sooner did the case of the Mashed Potato Murderess end than the case of the Serial Bread Squeezer began.

The first case ended on September 19, when a jury in Judge Heckler's Doylestown courtroom found twenty-six-year-old Heather Marie Miller, a mother of four, guilty of trying to murder her husband, Kevin Miller, by poisoning his mashed potatoes with belladonna in a scheme she devised with her next-door neighbor and alleged lesbian lover. It was a secret tape recording of the plot that led to Heather Miller's arrest. The recording was made by Mindi Robbins, the neighbor/lover, who alerted police to the plot. The two had discussed other ways of murdering Kevin Miller, including having him killed while dancing in a mosh pit at a rock concert.

For his part, Kevin Miller stood by his wife throughout the trial, frequently showing affection toward her. He said his wife was simply trying to get his attention because he worked two jobs from 8:00 A.M. until midnight almost every day. The jury found Heather Miller guilty and Judge Heckler sentenced her to four and a half to ten years in prison.

The very next day, Heckler began presiding over the trial of Samuel Feldman, an advertising salesman, and alleged bread squeezer and cookie crumbler. Feldman was accused of damaging 175 bags of bagels, 227 bags of potato dinner rolls, 3,087 loaves of Freihofer's sliced bread, and countless bags of Archway apricot and strawberry cookies over a two-year period at a Lower Makefield supermarket. Feldman was arrested and charged after security cameras set up in the bread aisle of the Giant food store showed him fondling loaves of bread and bags of cookies, three or four times a night on four consecutive nights. Feldman's lawyer, Ellis Klein, argued that his client was simply a picky shopper trying to find the freshest loaf of bread the way a lot of shoppers do. In one videotaped sequence, Feldman stands in the bread aisle with his wife, Sharon; when she turns away he reaches for a loaf and squeezes it while she's not looking.

A representative of Freihofer's claimed that Feldman had damaged $7,100 worth of bread (he kept returning to Freihofer's). Archway claimed he'd damaged $800 worth of its product. The jury found Feldman guilty of cookie crumbling but not guilty on the other counts. Judge Heckler threw out the jury verdict, however, and found Feldman guilty on both counts of criminal mischief. Before issuing a verdict, the judge ordered Feldman to undergo psychiatric counseling. In his subsequent ruling, Judge Heckler said he was disturbed by Feldman's comment to the psychiatrist that the "real bread squeezer" was probably still out on the loose. "The statement that some other person in the area had been doing this damage and that you just happened to wander into the crosshairs of a security camera at the same time is inconsistent with the jury's finding, and I don't believe it," Heckler told Feldman. He was sentenced to 180 days of probation and $1,000 restitution to the manufacturers, plus, almost needless to say, ongoing psychiatric counseling. "I do have a problem," Feldman admitted to the court. "Anytime I go shopping, my wife will supervise and will be with me."

## WHERE THE BLOB FIRST OOZED
### Chester County

POLICE LIEUTENANT DAVE: "Just because some kid smashes into your wife on the turnpike doesn't make it a crime to be seventeen."

That line from the 1958 movie *The Blob* should have been enough to alert viewers that this wasn't just another B horror movie, it was a teenage angst B horror movie. Why won't grown-ups *listen* when we tell them there's a flesh-absorbing ball of goo rolling around the Pennsylvania countryside?!

*The Blob* was Steve McQueen's first starring movie role and he played—what else?—a teenager who is on a lover's lane with his girlfriend when a meteor crashes nearby. They go to investigate, but a hobo finds the crash site first. He pokes the meteor with a stick and it breaks open to reveal a clear gooey center, which quickly leaps onto the hobo's hand. That's when Steve McQueen and his girlfriend find him screaming on the side of the road. They rush him to the local doc, and soon the hobo, the doctor, and Nurse Kate have all been blobsorbed.

The rest of the movie consists of McQueen and his teenage buddies trying to wake up authorities to the otherworldly menace. By the time of the movie's climax, the rolling ball of blood red silicone is as big as a house, or at least the Downingtown Diner, which the Blob is oozing over when McQueen discovers it can be stopped by cold. (In the end, they parachute a crate holding The Blob onto an Arctic ice floe. The credits read THE END with a big question mark.)

*The Blob* was one of the great horror classics of the late '50s. It was filmed entirely in Montgomery and Chester Counties by Valley Forge Films in Yellow Springs. Something of a Blob cult has formed and there are pilgrimages to famous Blob sites, such as the Downington Diner and the Colonial movie theater in Phoenixville, where the Blob oozed through the projectionist's viewing holes and gummed up the audience during the "Midnight Spook Show."

A few years ago, thirty members of the Horror and Fantasy Film Society of Baltimore took a Blob tour led by Wes Shank, a Montgomery County resident who purchased the actual Blob— a five-gallon container of red silicone used as an animated prop in the movie—from Valley Forge Films in 1965. In addition to the Colonial theater and the Downingtown Diner (the original has been torn down, but another was built on the same site), the Blob tourists visited what is now a Meineke Discount Mufflers shop in Phoenixville where the Blob ate a mechanic working under a car. Also on the tour was Jerry's Supermarket (now the "I Got It at Gary's" drugstore) on Lewis Road in Royersford, where Steve McQueen and his girlfriend hid in the walk-in refrigerator to escape the Blob. "The average person probably thinks we're a bunch of crazed fanatics, which we probably are," said Wes Shank during the Blob tour. "But it's all in good fun."

*The National Watch and Clock Museum is in the city of Columbia in Lancaster County. Columbia, on the Susquehanna River, could've been a contender—it was almost the capital of the United States. Congress voted instead to create a permanent location for the federal government in the region around the banks of the Potomac River, and named it District of Columbia.*

## A REAL PAIN IN THE NECK
### Darby

To people around the world, sixty-two-year-old Shirley Petrich of Delaware County became known as "the lady with the knife in her neck." To the people in her Colwyn neighborhood, Petrich's story became something of a pain in the neck because it gave the suburban Philadelphia community a black eye. In the process, Petrich became a symbol of urban apathy, a latter-day Kitty Genovese, the young New York woman whose cries for help as she was being murdered were ignored by her neighbors in Queens in the 1960s because they "didn't want to get involved." Fortunately, Shirley Petrich's story is more bizarre than tragic.

On March 3, 2000, Petrich left her house around six o'clock in the morning to do some errands. Petrich, who walked everywhere, had already dropped off papers at the recycling plant about three miles from her house and was on her way to the Acme supermarket in nearby Yeadon when an unidentified man ran up behind her, punched her in the back of the neck, and then ran off. At least that's what Petrich thought. But she hadn't been punched, she'd been stabbed, and the knife with the five-inch blade and wooden handle was sticking out of the back of her neck. Amazingly, Petrich didn't feel the knife when she rubbed her neck, nor did she return home or call the police. Instead, she continued on her way to the Acme, where surveillance cameras show her walking up and down the aisles with a knife clearly sticking out of the back of her neck. And nobody said anything to her because either they didn't notice or they "didn't want to get involved."

At least that was the spin put on the story by newspapers and TV outlets around the world. The footage of the Acme cameras and other security cameras outside showed Petrich pushing her shopping cart down the street with the knife clearly visible sticking out of the back of her neck. It wasn't until she had returned home and was changing her clothes to take a shower when her grown daughter noticed the knife and pulled it out. Petrich was rushed to the Hospital of the University of Pennsylvania, where she was treated and later released in good condiditon.

For the next several days, local radio talk shows and newspaper letters to the editor raged about society's indifference. How could someone *not* notice a knife in someone else's neck? Which begged the question, How could someone not know she had a knife in her *own* neck? A University of Pennsylvania sociologist called the incident an "extreme case of civil inattention." (The next time you see someone walking down the street with an arrow through his head, don't think it's a Steve Martin gag.) The only person who apparently noticed Petrich's unlikely dilemma was a child at a school crossing at Fourth and Pine Streets in Colwyn as the elderly woman with the shopping cart walked past on her way home. "What's in that lady's back?" asked the little girl. The crossing guard, Carol Zimmerman, looked up to see Petrich about 50 feet away with what looked like a piece of wood sticking out from her neck. "I had no idea it was a knife until I saw it on the news," Zimmerman said.

For her part, Shirley Petrich kept mum in the days and weeks that followed. Her daughter advised her not to speak to any reporters until someone agreed to pay. About six weeks later, the TV show *Inside Edition* paid Petrich $10,000 for her exclusive story. "It worked out well for me because I'm taking that money and moving out of Colwyn," said Petrich.

*BERKS COUNTY'S*
*MUSEUM OF CHILDHOOD*
*Douglassville*

**M**ary Merritt and her husband, Robert, were collectors.
Over a fifty-year period they collected enough antique
dolls and toys and knickknacks and geegaws and gnomes and
other interesting "stuff" to fill a museum. Two museums, in
fact: the Museum of Childhood and Mary Merritt's Doll
Museum. You can visit both of them where they sit side-by-side
on the Benjamin Franklin Highway (Route 422) midway
between Reading and Pottstown in Douglassville, Berks
County.

Mary Merritt's Doll Museum opened in 1963, and is filled
with the antique and collectible dolls she and her husband
found during the trips around the United States and Europe.
The museum is located in the back of the building, and contains what I am told is a remarkable collection of American
dolls from the 1850s to 1910, although there are dolls from
ancient Egypt up through modern times as well. There are
elaborate dollhouses and forty miniature rooms filled with
miniature furniture. Wouldn't you know that this was not one
of the trips I made without my daughter Molly.

There are mechanical dolls and Shirley Temple dolls and
Dionne quintuplet dolls and Barbie dolls and even G.I. Joe
dolls. In the front of the building is a doll shop where you can
purchase antique china dolls or offbeat collectibles, like a Robin
Williams Mork doll or a Pee Wee Herman pull-the-ring talking
doll (I was afraid to pull the ring to find out what he said).

Across the driveway is the Museum of Childhood, which
opened a year after Mary Merritt's Doll Museum, and which
could probably be called "The Museum of All The Other Stuff

*Mary Merritt's Doll Museum—did somebody say* dolls?

the Merritts Collected Over the Years." In fact, its original
name was Merritts' Early Americana Museum, which they built
to hold their vast collection of "remembrances of bygone eras."
If this is a museum of childhood, it certainly is a childhood no
one living today enjoyed. There weren't too many kids in my
neighborhood who grew up playing with whalebone scrimshaw
and pewter plates and garden gnomes, which seem to take up a
great deal of space in the museum. There are some quaint
mechanical toys from the early to mid–twentieth century: metal
fire engines with working ladders, World War II vintage air-
planes with propellers that spin, that sort of thing.

The Museum of Childhood, for some reason, includes tableaux of historical figures, such as Presidents Abraham Lincoln, Andrew Jackson, and Ulysses S. Grant sitting around a table. Clearly not included as part of it, but hard to miss above the heads of the presidents, is a child's drum set featuring Mickey and Minnie Mouse, Donald Duck, and Goofy on the front of the big bass drum. There's something very goofy about that, but then childhood can be like that.

Both museums are open 10:00 A.M. to 4:30 P.M. on weekdays except Tuesdays and from 1:00 to 5:00 P.M. on Sundays. The Museum of Childhood can be reached at (610) 385–3408, Mary Merritt's Doll Museum at (610) 385–3809.

## THE GERMAN CONNECTION
### Ephrata

**W**hen William Penn declared his province of Pennsylvania to be a "free-religion zone," in the lingo of today, no group of people took him up on his offer more than members of various German Christian sects with names like Amish, Mennonite, Moravian, Schwenkfelder, and others who fall under the larger group name *Brethren*. There are more than twenty Brethren groups, each an offshoot of another, the result of disagreements over various issues of faith.

The repression of their faith at home brought these German immigrants to Pennsylvania. The followers of Mennos Simons, a Dutch Roman Catholic priest who broke away from the church in 1536 over the issue of infant baptism, settled in Germantown, now part of the city of Philadelphia, in 1683. These Mennonites were called Pennsylvania Dutch because of the birthplace of their founder, but they were German-speaking, as were members of the Amish Church, a more conservative group within the Mennonite Church, founded in the 1690s.

Germantown was just what it sounded like—a town full of Germans—and in 1729 the German Christians in Northwest Philadelphia were joined by one hundred immigrants of a new religious order called Schwarzenau Brethren (Church of the Brethren or Dunkers), led by Alexander Mack. In 1732 a conservative and charismatic member of Mack's Brethren order broke away to form a cloister of celibate members (German Seventh Day Baptists) in Ephrata, Lancaster County. In 1740 a group of German missionaries, followers of the Bohemian priest John Hus, who was burned at the stake as a heretic in 1415, settled first in Nazareth and later Bethlehem. The called their church Unitas Fratrum (Latin for Unity of the Brethren) and intended to convert Native Americans and black slaves to Christianity. They were all Germans, but were called Moravians because they took refuge in Moravia during a period of persecution.

Another group, the Schwenkfelders, arrived in Philadelphia in 1734 and settled in Montgomery County along the Perkiomen Creek. The group takes its name from a pious German nobleman, Caspar Schwenckfeld von Ossig, a contemporary and early supporter of Martin Luther and the Reformation. But Schwenckfeld found the direction of Luther's Protestantism to be as extreme and exclusionary in its own way as the Catholic Church. His controversial writings toward a more ecumenical "Middle Way" of Reformation led to his exile. After his death in 1561, followers of his ideas increased in number until religious persecution drove them from Europe to America. The loosely organized Schwenkfelders did not become a Society until 1782 and the Schwenkfelder Church did not officially exist until 1909. Today there are five Schwenkfelder Churches—four in Montgomery County and one in Philadelphia—with a total congregation of 2,800. The most famous Schwenkfelder is probably Pennsylvania's former U.S.

Senator Richard Schweiker, who also served as Secretary of Health and Human Services under President Ronald Reagan.

Although their numbers are small today, the influence of these early religious immigrants from Germany can be seen throughout the Eastern Pennsylvania. Bethlehem, Nazareth, and Lititz were all founded by the Moravians, and until the 1850s only members of that faith could live in those closed communities. Bethlehem continues to be the administrative capital of the Northern Province of the Moravian Church in the United States. There are approximately 18,000 Moravians in Pennsylvania attending services at twenty-six churches throughout the state. The Moravians continue their missionary work; in fact, the largest Moravian community is on the African continent.

The Amish and Mennonites have spread throughout the country, but the largest numbers are found in Pennsylvania, Ohio, and Indiana. Lancaster County is the center of Amish Country, where their private and separate lifestyles have become a major tourist attraction. Most laymen can't tell the difference between Amish and Mennonite dress, but if you see an Amish-looking guy driving a car, he's a Mennonite.

The cloister formed in 1732 at Ephrata is empty now (you might expect this from a celibate religious order). After the death of founder Conrad Beissel in 1768, the number of white-robed brothers and sisters dwindled from a high of 300 to 135 in 1770. The Seventh Day German Baptist Church, as it was incorporated in 1814, managed to struggle on with a handful of followers until it dissolved in 1934. The grounds and gothic European buildings of the Ephrata Cloister were taken over by the Pennsylvania Historical and Museum Commission in 1941 and today is a National Historical Landmark. The cloister is open for tours showing the spartan nature of monastic life. (Ephrata Cloister, open 9:00 A.M. to 5:00 P.M. Monday through Saturday, and Sunday noon to 5:00 P.M.; admission charged; 717–733–6600. The mailing address is 642 W. Main Street, Ephrata, PA 17522.)

## THE LITTLE CHURCH
*Glenmoore*

"**W**hat is it we're looking for, Dad?" asked my ten-year-old daughter, Molly. "We're looking for the smallest church in the world," I told her. "What does it look like?" she asked. I hadn't a clue. In fact, I didn't know if it even existed. I had been told by a newspaper-delivery-truck driver about what he described as "the smallest church in the world" off Route 282 in Glenmoore, Chester County. "You can't miss it," the truck driver told me.

Famous last words if ever I've heard them. The *biggest* church in the world, now maybe that you can't miss. I drove through Glenmoore the first time without realizing that that little cluster of buildings I passed a while back was, in fact, a town. Then I went through it a second time (it looks different coming from the other direction).

Downtown Glenmoore consists of an intersection with no traffic light and one antiques shop next to a convenience store, where I stopped to ask for directions.

"Excuse me, guys," I said to the two teenagers behind the counter, "there's supposed to be a really, really small church around here. Have you ever heard of it?" They both shook their heads. I was half backing out the screen door when one boy said, "You mean *really* small?" I nodded. He pointed down Route 282. "It's a couple of miles that way on your right. But be careful, it's real easy to miss," he said. "It's about as big as a car."

For the record, it's about the size of a one-car garage or a big toolshed, if toolsheds were made out of flagstone. Also for

the record, The Little Church, as the sign outside describes
itself, is located in Cornog Crossing, another one-intersection
town about two miles south of Glenmoore, where Marshall
Road crosses Route 282. The kid at the convenience store was
right, you'd pass right by it if you didn't know where it was.
The Little Church is nestled under trees just six steps from the
roadway. Whether it's the smallest church in the world is an
issue best left to Mr. Ripley, but it's the smallest one I've ever
seen—about big enough for three people plus an altar. It's big
enough for a really intimate wedding, which it has been used
for on occasion, according to Dorothy Lambert at the Exxon
station across the street.

The sign outside the church reads: THE LITTLE CHURCH,
1928, FRANCISCO GASPARIA CANNELLA. BORN PALERMO, ITALY, 1875.
DIED 1952. The story behind it is a sweet one. Francisco Cannella came here from Italy to work the nearby quarry in the
1920s. Like many immigrants, he left his wife and children
behind, determined to work and save until he had raised
enough money to bring them all to America. Francisco went
one better. He made a promise to God that he would go to
church every day if God would allow him to bring his family
from Italy. God and Francisco's hard work paid off. The only
problem was that in order for Francisco to honor his pledge, he
had to travel nine miles to the nearest Catholic church in
Downtingtown in all kinds of weather on a dangerously winding road. But the Italian stonemason was a man of his word, so
he built the Little Church with his own hands, and each day
until the day he died he went there to thank God for bringing
his family to America.

Francisco's children still live in the house behind the Little
Church. Upon hearing the inspiring story of a father's love
and faith, my own darling child commented, "Can we go
home *now?!*"

## THE KEYSTONE CHINA SYNDROME
### *Harrisburg*

In March of 1979, *The China Syndrome*, starring Jane
Fonda, Michael Douglas, and Jack Lemmon, opened in movie
theaters around the country. The movie dealt with a fictional
accident at a nuclear power station; its title came from the
notion that a meltdown in a nuclear reactor would burn a hole
through the earth all the way to China. In reality, a character
in the movie says, a meltdown of a nuclear reactor would burn
a hole through the earth until it hit groundwater, sending
plumes of radioactive steam into the air that would "contami-
nate an area the size of Pennsylvania." Two weeks later the real
thing happened at Three Mile Island Nuclear Power Station
near Harrisburg.

At 4:07 A.M. on March 28, 1979, the alarm sirens began
wailing at the TMI facility on an island in the middle of the
Susquehanna River. A faulty valve had allowed air to enter the
cooling system, causing the nuclear reactor core to overheat.
Sixty-nine baron rods smashed into the reactor core to stop the
nuclear fission, but it was too late. The worst commercial
nuclear power accident in American history was under way.
The temperature reached 4,300 degrees inside the reactor core
in Unit One of Three Mile Island's two nuclear reactors. At a
temperature of 5,300 degrees a China Syndrome meltdown
would have taken place as the nuclear material burned through
the containment vessel into the riverbed. Pennsylvania was
spared its own Chernobyl by a matter of degrees.

The images of the accident at Three Mile Island are unforget-
table. Mass evacuations. Headlines about a huge hydrogen bubble.
President Jimmy Carter padding around in ridiculous-looking

paper decontamination slippers on a visit to the plant. It was all quite scary, but you'd never know it on a visit to Three Mile Island twenty-some years later. Unit One has been shut down ever since that day, but Unit Two is still churning out the nuclear heat that boils the water that turns the turbines that produce electricity for much of central Pennsylvania. Two of the four 372-foot-tall cooling towers still spew ominous-looking but benign clouds of mist. The towers dominate the Dauphin County landscape the way City Hall Tower once dominated Philadelphia. But there's no William Penn statue atop these cooling towers, only the misty memories of what might have been.

Like the Knox Mine Disaster, which drove a stake through the heart of Pennsylvania's deep anthracite mining industry, the accident at Three Mile Island not only crippled the commercial nuclear power generating movement in Pennsylvania, it ended it in the United States. No nuclear generating station has been built in America since the accident.

Today you can have your picture taken with the TMI cooling towers looming like boogeymen overhead. The TMI Visitors Center is located across the street from the power plant on Route 441 near Middletown. Hours are limited—noon to 4:30 P.M. Thursday through Sunday—and it's closed January and February. Call the TMI switchboard at (717) 948–8000 to check seasonal hours.

## CHOCOLATE CITY, USA
### *Hershey*

**W**hat Philadelphia means to liberty, what Pittsburgh means (meant) to steel, what Heinz means to ketchup, the town of Hershey means to (a) kisses, (b) bars, (c) orphans, (d) choco-

late. You have thirty seconds to answer. No, make that fifteen.
In fact, time's up.

The answer, of course, is all of the above. Hershey symbol-
izes many things to many people, not the least of which is the
bittersweet subject of orphans. And behind it all is the name
Milton S. Hershey, the candy-making visionary who created a
factory town and a product famous all over the earth.

The Hershey Bar is an American icon born and raised, like
its inventor and namesake, in Central Pennsylvania, just a
stone's throw from the state capital, Harrisburg. Born in 1857
in the village of Derry Church to a devout Mennonite family,
young Milton Snavely Hershey completed a formal education
only through fourth grade. He worked first as a printer's
apprentice and then as a candy maker's apprentice. At at the
age of 18 he moved to Philadelphia to open a candy shop,
which failed after six years. Hershey moved to Denver, then
Chicago, then New Orleans, then New York City, trying in each
city to establish a successful candy-making business. In 1883,
he returned to Lancaster, Pennsylvania, where he incorporated
the candy-making techniques he had learned in his travels, key
among them the use of fresh milk in the making of caramel.
His Lancaster Caramel Co. was a success, and in 1893 he purchased new German-manufactured candy coating machines,
which he later used to manufacture his recipe for a milk chocolate candy bar he would name Hershey.

In 1900 Milton Hershey sold his caramel candy business for
a tidy sum of one million dollars. He used the money to move
back to his birthplace of Derry Church, where he built the
largest chocolate factory in the world. So successful was the
Hershey Chocolate Co., and so generous and foresighted was
Milton Hershey—he built employee housing of a quality-of-life
design never seen before, as well as an inexpensive public
transportation system to allow employees to live in nearby
towns—that Derry Church was renamed Hershey.

In 1909, Milton Hershey and his wife, Catherine, who had no children of their own, established a trade school for orphaned boys. In 1918, three years after the premature death of his wife, Hershey placed his entire fortune of $60 million in a trust fund for the support of his school for orphans. Today the Milton S. Hershey School has a residential enrollment of 1,500 financially needy boys and girls between the ages of four and eighteen, no longer orphans necessarily, who live on a 10,000-acre campus. Milton Hershey, who lived to a ripe old age of eighty-eight, was technically penniless at the time of his death in 1945. Penniless but rich beyond measure, having given away all his wealth and assured the future education of countless thousands. And it only gets better. In 1963 the Hershey School Trust donated $50 million to establish the Milton S. Hershey Medical Center and the Hershey College of Medicine, which opened in 1967.

Meanwhile, the business Hershey founded thrived, as did the city bearing his name. In the 1930s during the Great Depression, Milton Hershey launched a building program to make sure his employees still had work. They constructed a grand hotel, a sports arena, a community center, and a new corporate headquarters. Later, the gardens and public park and zoo that Hershey built with corporate funds were developed into one of the most popular theme parks in the United States. Hershey, Pennsylvania, is now a destination for families seeking fun and sweets, a Chocolate Disneyland with streetlights that look like Hershey Kisses.

Hershey Bars may be an American icon, but the unlikely yarn of Milton Hershey, the kid with the fourth-grade education who persevered through failure to establish one of the great business and philanthropic empires in the United States, is a true Pennsylvania success story equal to that of Stephen Girard, John Wanamaker, and Andrew Carnegie. A sweet story about a sweet man, a nice guy who finished first.

# SOMETHING ABOUT CHOCOLATE

*Some chocolate trivia,*
*courtesy of the Hershey Chocolate Co.*
*Answers below.*

1. What year was chocolate invented? By whom?
2. What is the most important ingredient in chocolate?
3. Name some countries where cacao beans are produced.
4. How many pounds of cacao beans are stored in the silos at the Hershey Chocolate Company?
5. Name four things that must be in chocolate for it to be called chocolate.
6. How many pounds of milk does the factory use in one day?
7. How many people toured the chocolate factory before it ended tours in 1973?
8. In what year were Hershey Kisses introduced?
9. How many kisses can be produced at the Hershey plant in one day?
10. What are the names of the two main streets in Hershey?
11. What is the ideal temperature for storing chocolate?
12. At what temperature does chocolate melt?

*Answers to Hershey trivia:*

1. *1528, by the Spanish*
2. *Cacao beans*
3. *Ghana, Ecuador, Jamaica, Costa Rica, Mexico, Cameroon*
4. *90 million pounds*
5. *Sugar, chocolate liquor, cocoa butter, condensed milk*
6. *Almost one million*
7. *10 million*
8. *1907*
9. *24 million*
10. *Chocolate Avenue and Cocoa Avenue*
11. *65 degrees Fahrenheit*
12. *78 degrees Fahrenheit*

## THE GRINCH WHO STOLE
## WILT CHAMBERLAIN'S BALL
### Hershey

Like Woodstock, New York, was to a generation of long-haired hippies in 1969, Hershey, Pennsylvania, was to a generation of Philadelphia basketball fans in 1962. People everywhere say they were there. The difference between the three days of music at Woodstock and the night Wilt Chamberlain of the Philadelphia Warriors scored one hundred points against the New York Knicks was about a half million people. There were only about 5,000 people present at the Hershey Arena on March 2, 1962, the night Wilt made history and set an NBA record that no one has come close to touching almost four decades later.

For the record, I was not one of the 5,000. I was at home listening to Bill Campbell's play-by-play on the radio in my brother's bedroom with my grade-school friend Dave Brennan. The closer Wilt got to one hundred points, the more desperately the Knicks tried to stop him—double- and triple-teaming him. They knew the record books would always include the New York Knickerbockers as the opponent that a single player scored an impossible one hundred points against. They did not succeed.

One basketball fan who *was* present that night was fourteen-year-old Kerry Ryman, who was lurking near courtside when Wilt scored his one hundredth point with forty-six seconds left in the game. The referee blew the whistle after his historic shot and fans rushed onto the court. Ryman was one of them. He grabbed the ball and ran up the stairs, out of the arena, with a security guard in hot pursuit. Or so the story goes.

Ryman, of nearby Annville, did what any kid would do with a souvenir ball back in those pre-big-bucks-for-sports-memorabilia days. He played with it for years. Then he put it in his closet, where it sat in a plastic bag until Chamberlain's death at the age of sixty-three on October 12, 1999. The next day's *York Dispatch* had a story about the guilt that Ryman, now a crane operator, felt all these years for having stolen the ball. "If I had the chance to do it over again, I never would have taken the ball," Ryman said the day Wilt died. "If I could get $1 million for it, I wouldn't want it. I was there and saw what Wilt the Stilt did. That's what has meaning to me."

Funny what happens to meaning when money is involved. Within months of Chamberlain's death, Ryman's one-hundred-point-ball was up for bids at Leland auction house in New York, where it sold to an unidentified sports enthusiast for $551,844. No sooner had the sale been announced than questions arose as to the authenticity of Ryman's claim. Warriors and later Seventy-Sixers statistician Harvey Pollack was at the game. "I saw Willie Smith, the referee, who's now dead, give it [the one-hundred-point ball] to Tommy McCoy, the trainer, who gave it to Jeff Millman, the equipment manager. He took the ball and put it in Wilt's duffel bag in the locker room. They finished the game, the last forty-six seconds, with a replacement ball."

The questions of authenticity led to the sale being voided by the auction house in May 2000. In October, the suspect ball went up for auction again, this time with full disclosure as to its dubious legitimacy. How much would you be willing to pay for a record-setting piece of sports history with more question marks on it than The Riddler? An unnamed East Coast sports memorabilia dealer felt the debatable B-ball was worth $67,791, of which Ryman got $59,000, approximately $431,000 less than he would have gotten from the original auction. "What happened?" Ryman asked afterward. "Why would someone bid $500,000 the first time and then nothing?" I guess you had to be there.

## PENNSYLVANIA'S BACHELOR PRESIDENT
### Lancaster

The only Pennsylvanian to become President of the United States is best remembered for being the chief executive who preceded Abraham Lincoln in the White House. Under James Buchanan, the United States inched inexorably toward Civil War, even though he was considered a pro-South president. His one term in office was marked by the Supreme Court's dreadful Dred Scott Decision, which Buchanan considered binding as law. Dred Scott was a slave who escaped to a free state and who sought legal protection in the courts. Ultimately, the Supreme Court ruled that slaves had no rights as citizens, even on free soil. No historian ranks Buchanan among the nation's best presidents, and some would argue that he deserves to be listed among the worst. Perhaps it's only a coincidence, but in Buchanan's hometown of Lancaster, Buchanan Avenue begins where Lemon Street ends.

Buchanan was America's only bachelor president; his niece, Harriet Lane, performed the hostess duties of the First Lady. His failure to marry alone would be enough to start tongues wagging as to Buchanan's sexual preferences, although he has been "outed" in many gay publications in recent years because of his long-term relationship with William R. King, a senator from Alabama who died while serving as Vice President of the United States under Buchanan's predecessor, Franklin Pierce. Buchanan and King shared a room at a Washington, D.C., boardinghouse for several years while each served in Congress. One of President James Polk's law partners derisively labeled the two roommates "Mr. and Mrs. Buchanan." Several politicians referred to King as Buchanan's "better half" and President Andrew Jackson was known to call King "Miss Nancy" or "Aunt Fancy."

*Wheatland, in Lancaster, home of Pennsylvania's only president, James Buchanan.*

Buchanan's estate, Wheatland, is open for tours in the city of Lancaster. The grand brick Victorian country home is decorated with souvenirs from Buchanan's days as envoy to Russia and ambassador to Great Britain, including signed portraits of Queen Victoria and Prince Albert. Still intact at Wheatland is the back porch where Buchanan was sitting in June 1856 when the news arrived that he had won the Democratic nomination for President. Fanning himself in the summer heat and sitting in shirtsleeves, Buchanan made a brief acceptance speech. Buchanan once wrote that the only reason he went into politics was "as a distraction from a great grief which happened at Lancaster when I was a young man." The grief was the death of his former fiancée, Anne C. Coleman, who died shortly after breaking off the engagement for unknown reasons.

Wheatland is open daily from April through November; closed Easter and Thanksgiving Day. Call (717) 392–8721.

## MAIN LINE RHYMES
### The Main Line

P hiladelphia's Main Line is string of suburban neighborhoods running west of the city along the Main Line of the
Pennsylvania Railroad. What Larchmont is to New York, what
Grosse Point is to Detroit, what Beverly Hills is to Los Angeles,
the Main Line is to Philadelphia. More blue blood than blue collar, the traditional Main Line is the C. K. Dexter Haven and
Tracey Davenport old-money Philadelphia portrayed in *The
Philadelphia Story*. In fact, Katharine Hepburn is an alumnae
of Bryn Mawr College, one of the Main Line's (and the nation's)
most prestigious institutions of higher education. In inter-
views, Hepburn would often mention through her trademark
clenched teeth that, after all, "I am a Bryn Mawr girl."

Today the Main Line is indistinguishable from any other
wealthy suburb when seen from a car traveling along Route 30
(Lancaster Avenue). But within a few blocks in any direction
can be found some of the grandest mansions and gated estates
this side of Buckingham Palace. To get a flavor, turn right off
of Montgomery Avenue at the Merion Cricket Club and mean-
der among the swells.

Most of the towns along the Main Line were renamed by the
president of the Pennsylvania Railroad in the 1890s. Pennsy
President George Roberts named his train stations after towns
in his ancestral home Wales. The train station in Elm was called
Narberth, the one in Athensville was called Ardmore, the one in
Humphreysville was called Bryn Mawr, and so forth. Technically, the communities voted to change their names to the same
names as the train stations, but it was more out of self-defense.

Ironically, the one community without a Welsh name gives
its name to the famous commuter train that serves the Main

Line—the Paoli Local. Paoli, the western end of the original Main Line about 20 miles from Center City, is named after Corsican patriot Pasquale Paoli (actually, it's named after a tavern named for the Corsican patriot).

There's a way that Philadelphians with too much time on their hands remember the order of the towns along the Main Line. It's a mnemonic, two of them actually. The first goes: Old Maids Never Wed And Have Babies (Overbrook, Merion, Narberth, Wynnewood, Ardmore, Haverford, Bryn Mawr). The second one is a bit more labored: Really Viscious Retrievers Snap Willingly, Snarl Dangerously. Beagles Don't, Period (Rosemont, Villanova, Radnor, St. Davids, Wayne, Strafford, Devon, Berwyn, Daylesford, Paoli).

S T I L L   A   T O U G H   T I C K E T   T O   G E T

*Merion*

B y all reports and documentary evidence, Albert Barnes
was a cranky young man who grew into cranky old man-
hood while amassing a fortune with which he purchased artwork valued, conservatively, at $3 billion. Barnes grew up in
Kensington, one of Philadelphia's crankiest working-class
neighborhoods. He brought the chip on his shoulder and his
collection of art to his home in Montgomery County, where it
has been giving the art world and the neighborhood fits ever
since the Barnes Foundation opened in 1922 at 300 North
Latches Lane in Merion.

Barnes was brilliant as well as ornery. He graduated from
the University of Pennsylvania's Medical School in 1892 at
the age of twenty. As a young man, Dr. Albert Barnes developed a patent medicine called Argyrol, an antiseptic, which he
manufactured and which made him a millionaire many times
over. In 1913 Barnes began collecting art seriously. By 1920
he owned the largest collection of Renoirs outside of France,
along with works by Cézanne, Matisse, Seurat, van Gogh,
Picasso, Gaugin, Degas, Rousseau, Manet, Miró, Cassatt, Cha-
gall, Pissaro, Titian, El Greco, Goya, Reubens, Delacroix, Dau-
mier, Modigliani, van Goyen, and Toulouse-Lautrec, among
others. Then Barnes hung his thousand paintings on the
walls of his house—dozens of them per wall, stacked almost
from floor to ceiling—and he placed his hundreds of pieces of
sculpture in these same rooms. Then he dared anyone to actually come and see them.

At least, that's the way it seemed to the art world that
wanted to flock to the Barnes Foundation he created in 1922.
Albert Barnes had his own ideas about how his art should be

presented and who should see it. He wanted students, not crit-
ics or admirers. He had developed a scientific approach to the
appreciation of art, and he wanted his art classes to reflect his
theories. His classes were open to anyone, but his collection
was not. You couldn't "drop by" the Barnes Foundation. And
what you would find if you did were countless masterpieces
unidentified by artist or period or subject but arranged on the
walls to reflect the scientific principles of art—space, line,
color, light, and focus—that Barnes wanted to express by his
individual choices.

His will forbade any changes in the way his art was displayed, and after his death in a car accident in 1951 at the
age of seventy-eight, the first of several lawsuits were filed
seeking greater public access to the priceless Barnes collection. In 1961 the lawsuits filed by the *Philadelphia Inquirer*
and the state of Pennsylvania were settled out of court, and
the Barnes Foundation agreed to open its doors to the public—reservations required months ahead of time—two days a
week.

Since then the collection has been made even more available to the public, which resulted in lawsuits brought by
neighbors trying to prevent tour buses from parking in the
leafy neighborhood. Even the Board of the Barnes Foundation has gone to court seeking to overturn Albert Barnes's
restrictive rules regarding how the art should be displayed.
In 1992 a court ruling allowed a onetime world tour of some
of the Barnes masterpieces to raise money for the upkeep of
the collection.

The Barnes collection includes 180 works by Renoir,
sixty-nine by Cézanne, sixty by Matisse, forty-four by
Picasso, eighteen by Rousseau, and a mere seven by van
Gogh. The Barnes Foundation is open to the public three
days a week. Advance reservations are still required. Phone
610–667–0290. The mailing address is 300 N. Latch's Lane,
Merion, PA 19066.

## WHERE EDSELS GO TO DIE
### Oxford

When the Ford Motor Company decided to introduce an
automobile named for Henry Ford's son, Edsel, in 1957,
America was not ready for a car with a horse collar grille that
*Time* magazine described as "an Oldsmobile sucking a lemon."
The Edsel had a lot of neat technological advances, such as a
push-button transmission in the center of the steering wheel, but
the doomed model was so ugly that it was discontinued after
1960. Only 150,000 Edsels were manufactured during that time.

Hugh Lesley was a twenty-five-year-old farmer in 1957
when the Edsel was introduced. If it wasn't love at first sight it
was certainly an enduring love. Lesley couldn't afford a new
Edsel (they sold for $3,500) but in 1960 he managed to buy a
used 1958 Edsel convertible for $750. Then he bought an Edsel
station wagon. Then a sedan. By 1962 Lesley owned eight
Edsels. It was only the beginning. By the early 1990s Lesley
was being hailed as the owner of the world's largest collection
of Edsels. Today there are almost 175 Edsels, many of them
rusting hulks, scattered like the bones of an elephants' grave-
yard on Lesley's farm, Lemongrove, off Route 472 west of
Oxford in Chester County.

"A good running '58 can get about $10,000," Lesley said of
the Edsel collector's market. Most of his do not fall into the cat-
egory of "good running." He's got a few of the Edsels in better
condition under a roof in a big barnlike shed, but he estimates
only twenty "with a little work" are in running condition. His
collection is fairly famous among Edsel restoration circles, and
he gets an average of one phone call a week from someone

*Tourists can stand in the bronze footprints of Rocky Balboa at the top of the steps of the Philadelphia Art Museum, a spot made famous in the first Rocky movie. Rocky (Sylvester Stallone) leaped up and down in triumph here after running up the steps.*

seeking a hard-to-find replacement item. "I try to help out people who need parts," he explains.

Lesley's collection includes his first Edsel, which sits under a tarp outside. "I still have it, but it's all worn out," he says. Since 1992, his claim to owning the world's largest collection of Edsels has been surpassed by Leroy Walker of Beulah, North Dakota, who had more than 210 Edsels at last count. "He's got his spread all over the prairie," Lesley said, adding, "He's been here to see mine." You know how Edsel guys have to stick together.

### B I B L I C A L   P E N N S Y L V A N I A
#### P h i l a d e l p h i a

Although there are several Pennsylvania cities mentioned by name in the Bible—Nanty Glo, Pittsburgh, and Altoona being overlooked in some revised editions—only one rates a special mention regarding the end of human life as we know it. As you might expect, the authors of the Bible never actually *visited* the Lehigh or Delaware Valley, but they obviously anticipated these areas as fine locations for towns that would eventually bear the names Emmaus, Nazareth, Bethlehem, Bethel, Lebanon, and Philadelphia.

While Bethlehem and Nazareth get top billing in the New Testament's greatest hits, specifically in the four Gospels by the biblical Beatles, Matthew, Mark, Luke, and (the cute one) John, only Philadelphia is singled out for mention in what might be called "The Scariest Story Ever Told." In the Book of Revelation, which is the Bible's final word, so to speak, Philadelphia is mentioned as a key player in the end of the world (this, incidentally, before either Frank Rizzo or Wilson Goode had been elected mayor).

Revelation—or Revelations, as it is frequently called—concludes the second section of the Christian Bible. Except for Hollywood movie screenwriters and producers, it may be one of the least-read books in the New Testament, probably because it's full of fire and brimstone. For example: "Then I saw an angel standing in the sun; and he cried with a loud voice, saying to all the birds that fly in the midst of heaven, 'Come and gather together for the supper of the great God, that you may eat the flesh of kings, the flesh of captains, the flesh of mighty men, the flesh of horses and those who sit on them, and the flesh of all people, free and slave, both small and great.'" In Hollywood you could take a meeting and say, "Revelation? What's not to like? It's got Armageddon! It's got Apocalypse! It's got at least four guys on horses. And best of all, it's got murder, mayhem, trials, tribulations, seven seals, and the daily number of the millennium—666!"

Revelation deals with the Second Coming of Christ and certainly includes the first mention of Philadelphia in world literature. The author, St. John the Divine (who may or may not have been related to the cute one), wrote the story sometime during the first century as a prophetic letter to the seven churches of Asia, the sixth of which was Philadelphia, a city that is now called Amman, the capital of Jordan. (Question: Why would an ancient Palestinian town under Roman rule have a Greek name meaning "City of Brotherly Love"? Answer: Three words—Alexander the Great.)

John was acting as a reporter in Revelation, recording the sights and the voice instructions he received from Jesus, evidently in Greek because Jesus introduced himself by saying, "I am the Alpha and the Omega, the First and the Last." The specific messages to each of the seven churches in Asia include equal parts of praise, scolding, and prophecy. The instructions to Philadelphia (and one would hope the rest of Pennsylvania) include these words: "Because you have kept my command to persevere, I will also keep you from the hour of trial which shall come upon the whole world to test those who dwell on the earth. Behold, I am coming quickly! Hold fast what you have, that no one may take your crown."

# HERE'S
# LOOKING AT CHEW

*The last of a breed of realist painters died in Wheeling, West Virginia, on November 24, 2000, and with him passed a piece of Pennsylvania history. His name was Harley Warrick and you've probably seen his handiwork while driving along backroads or highways, along Route 30 between Gettysburg and Chambersburg, or Route 255 between Dubois and St. Mary's, or several places along the Pennsylvania Turnpike between Lancaster and Somerset Counties. Wherever you've seen a* CHEW MAIL POUCH TOBACCO *sign on the side of a barn, you've probably seen Warrick's brush strokes.*

*Harley Warrick wasn't the only man to paint Mail Pouch ads on barns throughout Pennsylvania and the Midwest, but by his reckoning, at the time of his death at the age of seventy-six he had painted or repainted 20,000 barns with the famous black, white, and yellow message* CHEW MAIL POUCH TOBACCO. TREAT YOURSELF TO THE BEST. *In the process he helped create and preserve a piece of vanishing Americana that is going the way of the dodo and Burma-Shave signs. Mail Pouch barns used to be as common as Sheetz convenience stores throughout Pennsylvania, but now you've got to keep your eyes peeled or you could miss the faded lettering on the side of the barn on Route 309 between Hazelton and Tamaqua.*

*"The first thousand were a little rough, and after that you got the hang of it," Warrick said in a 1997 interview, recounting his fifty-plus years painting Mail Pouch barns. He started working for Mail Pouch as a painter fresh out of the Army in 1946. He and a helper would travel the countryside, painting two barns a day, six days a week for a weekly salary of $32.*

*Mail Pouch Tobacco Co. started advertising on the sides of barns and other high-visibility buildings in the late 1800s. The original slogan was "Clean Lasting Chew" rather than "Treat Yourself to the Best." Thousands of barns were painted, from Pennsylvania to Oregon.*

*Mail Pouch Tobacco barns can still be seen along the Pennsylvania Turnpike,
and along backroads and highways in various parts of the state.*

The beginning of the end for Mail Pouch signs was the 1965
highway beautification act, which prohibited advertising within
660 feet of federal highways. Then came bans on tobacco
advertising. In 1969 the company discontinued the barn-painting
program but they kept Warrick working repainting existing
barns. By the time Mail Pouch barns achieved historic landmark
status, Warrick was something of a historic landmark himself. He
worked for Mail Pouch full-time until 1992; in his retirement, he
built and painted Mail Pouch barn birdhouses, bird feeders, and
mailboxes.

Today "Chew Mail Pouch" barns are becoming as rare as
brass spittoons or smoking sections in restaurants. There are still
perhaps a hundred in Pennsylvania, but fewer each year as time
and progress take their toll.

## ECW: THE E STANDS FOR EXTREME
### Philadelphia

t's like a rumble under the highway between rival gangs. No, it *is* a rumble under the highway between rival gangs, except the turf they are fighting over is a squared wrestling ring lined with barbed wire instead of ring ropes. It's a hot summer Saturday night in South Philly and the roar of the crowd can be heard from inside a gray, windowless, two-story cinder block warehouse wedged hard against the pillars of I–95. A few blocks away, the roar of a larger crowd can be heard soaring into the lighted sky above Veterans Stadium where the Phillies are playing the Dodgers. But the chant rising from the menacing gloom under the highway tells a different story by different fans of a different sport. "We want blood! We want blood!"

Blood they want and blood they get. Tag team partners and real-life brothers Terry and Dory Funk are a bloody mess, their long hair matted against their faces with red liquid oozing from their scalps where they were cut by the barbed wire or laid open by a smash to the head with a folding chair wielded by their opponents, Flyboy Rocco Rock and Johnny Grunge of Public Enemy, tag team champions of ECW (Extreme Championship Wrestling). The wrestlers have already tumbled out of the ring into the audience and then out the front door of the ECW Arena at Swanson and Ritner Streets. Outside, under the hum of tires and downshifting trucks overhead, the wrestlers bash each other with conveniently empty aluminum trash cans as the crowd pours out the doors to watch the street fight. In a few minutes, they crash back inside the arena and return to the barbed-wire ring, where the bloody Funk brothers are on the verge of not only losing the match but of needing a transfusion. The referee, who may as well have been doing on-line

*Over the years the owner and employees at Mid-City Tire in South Philadelphia have adopted so many stray cats that the city erected a cat crossing sign near the shop at 7th and Washington Avenue.*

stock purchases for all he mattered during most of the match, suddenly declares a disqualification. Victorious Public Enemy raise their arms in triumph. The hostile South Philly crowd of 1,200 responds by heaving folding chairs into the ring. Not one, not two, not ten. More than fifty folding chairs are thrown over the barbed wire into the ring until Public Enemy is literally buried under a sea of metal.

What a great night! And that, in a nutshell, is what turned an obscure Pennsylvania wrestling federation (originally called Eastern Championship Wrestling when it was founded in 1992) into a legitimate rival of the WWF (World Wrestling Federation) and the WCW (World Championship Wrestling). ECW matches are broadcast on the Turner Cable Network and pay-per-view cable, and according to ECW founder Tod Gordon, owner of an upscale pawn shop in Center City, the ECW in Japan is as hot as Jerry Lewis in France. "The ECW is considered the quote-unquote hottest property in wrestling right now," Gordon said.

The proof in that is how the WWF and the WCW have adopted some of the ECW's more extreme elements of hard-core violence. There's no way a 270-pound man can stand on top of the ring ropes and do a back flip out of the ring and land on his head on hard concrete without injuring himself. And that's exactly what happened to Sabu, a wrestler considered a maniac in a business of maniacs, when he back-flipped off the ring ropes in an attempt to crush ECW champion Shane "The Franchise" Douglas, who lay near unconsciousness on a table after being thrown out of the ring by Sabu. Douglas moved at the last instant, and Sabu crashed through the table and hit the concrete floor headfirst. Sabu was taken away on a stretcher. "No one's ever been able to stretcher this guy," says Gordon, as if "The Franchise" were responsible rather than the concrete floor.

Douglas, who has since moved back to the WWF, is a Pittsburgh native and former high school teacher whose real name is Troy Martin (no kidding). "I grew up watching Bruno Samartino and Nature Boy Buddy Rogers, that whole class of wrestler, when wrestling was wrestling instead of this cartoon that we see now on Saturday morning," Shane Douglas told me. "If I left no other mark on the business, I want to do it with ECW."

ECW has left its mark on the business. The cartoon stuff in the WWF began to harden up when ECW alumni like Steve "Stone Cold" Austin began moving up to the bigger-salaried wrestling league. The ECW arena is still under the highway in South Philly, and it still takes its show on the road to smaller auditoriums in Wilkes-Barre and Pittsburgh and Trenton. And that's the way ECW fans like it.

# NEVER TOO LATE TO JOIN
## Philadelphia

P hiladelphia has always been a clubby city. Per capita,
Philadelphia has more clubs than a deck of cards: sports
clubs, veterans' clubs, eating clubs, social clubs, Mummers'
clubs, ethnic clubs, political clubs, union clubs, military clubs,
professional clubs, and my personal favorite, ridiculous clubs.
Two of the most ridiculous clubs are the Friday the 13th Club
and the Procrastinators Club. We'll get to the Procrastinators
Club later.

The Friday the 13th Club was founded in 1936 by an advertising man named Phil Klein who understood that newspapers
and wire services love wacky stories with no redeeming social
value. So he created a club consisting of himself and clients
seeking publicity, who gathered each Friday the 13th to tempt
fate by opening umbrellas indoors, breaking mirrors, walking
under ladders, spilling salt, and allowing black cats to cross
their paths. The Friday the 13th Club held its meetings in various public places over the years—the zoo, the Market Street
subway, the Forrest Theater stage, the Belmont Avenue
entrance ramp to the Schuylkill Expressway—always on a Friday, always on the 13th of the month, and always called to
order promptly at 12:13 P.M.

The Friday the 13th Club met an average of once a year,
although there were multiple Friday the 13ths in 1942, 1974,
and 1996. Phil Klein, who died in 1982, had written a sunset
provision into the Friday the 13th Club by producing a calendar
that listed every Friday the 13th from 1936 through the year
2000, when the club would disband. "To give the world a break,
we should all be dead by 2001," wrote Klein in the club bylaws.

And so it was that on Friday, October 13, 2000, that the Friday the 13th Club held its final public function in the Swann

Fountain in Center City Philadelphia. Leading the festivities was Phil Klein's younger brother, Harry, age eighty-two, and Phil's son Arthur, age sixty-six. "Years of walking under ladders, throwing salt over your shoulder, it's no fun," said Arthur before the last meeting. "Maybe I'll get some luck now." Perhaps the greatest legacy of the Friday the 13th Club was making the word triskaidekaphobia (fear of the number 13) a common spelling bee word in Philadelphia schools.

And now on to the Procrastinators Club, which they got around to founding in 1956, and which has been led by acting president Les Waas since then because the club hasn't yet counted the votes from the 1957 club elections. Like Klein, Waas was an advertising man who saw a good idea and ran with it, if procrasinators ever actually run. The first meeting was scheduled for the Bellevue Stratford Hotel, and then postponed as a joke. The Philadelphia newspapers loved the idea and Waas contacted a bunch of friends to have an actual luncheon meeting of the Procrastinators Club, which began promptly at dinnertime.

Over the years club membership has grown to more than half a million, 5,000 of whom actually filled out the membership application, which says READ LATER on top. For dues of $12, members receive a License to Procrastinate plus a subscription to *Last Month's Newsletter*, which is published every twelve years. And what exactly is procrastination? "Procrastination is putting off till later those things which are not necessarily done immediately, and also putting off those things preferably we don't like to do, in the interest of those things eventually never needing to be done," explains Waas.

Over the years newspaper and radio stations have looked forward to reporting on the Procrastinators Club predictions for the new year, which are usually reported twelve months late. "We're the only people who have a 100 percent accuracy rate on our prognostications," Waas says. "Also we're the only people who can be called 'the late' so-and-so and still be around to hear it."

The club motto is the urgent message "Procrastinate Now!" and its national holiday is "Be Late for Something Day," held each year on the day after Labor Day. In 1980 when the Phillies won the World Series, the Procrastinators Club issued a proclamation congratulating the team for waiting ninety-seven years to win its first World Championship. In past presidential elections, the Procrastinators Club issued an early endorsement for Buchanan—James Buchanan, Pennsylvania's only president, elected in 1856. Why Buchanan, who died in 1868? "Because only live politicians cause deficits, high taxes, wars, etc." says Waas. "And dead presidents make better currency."

*THE DOCTOR IS OUT: street corner relationship counseling takes place on this bench at Second and Reed Streets in South Philadelphia when the doctor is in.*

## PENNSYLVANIANS IN HEAVEN
### Philadelphia

There are only four Americans officially canonized as saints in the Catholic Church, and two of them are from Philadelphia.

St. John Neumann was the Bishop of Philadelphia and the founder of the parochial school system in the United States. You can see him in the flesh, so to speak, in a glass coffin in the lower church of St. Peter's Church at Fifth Street and Girard Avenue in North Philadelphia. His remains were moved there in 1963 after the Pope declared him "Blessed," which is the last step before sainthood. St. John Neumann was canonized by Pope Paul VI in Rome in 1977, one hundred and seventeen years after his death in 1860. The Shrine of St. John Neumann, which houses his remains, includes a small museum that tells the story of his life. Also on display are various instruments of self-mortification worn by the saint during his life on earth, such as a hair shirt of coarse fibers that made every movement uncomfortable, and a "discipline" collar with sharp edges that made every turn of his head excruciating.

Mother Katherine Drexel, who was canonized on October 1, 2000, is entombed in Bensalem, Bucks County, inside the convent of the Sisters of the Blessed Sacrament, the religious order she founded in 1891. She died in 1955 at the age of ninety-six. Her path to sainthood was much faster than St. John Neumann's primarily because of the miracles attributed to her intercession in the relatively few years after her death. In 1974 Robert Gutherman, an altar boy who assisted in servicing Mass at the convent, was diagnosed with a debilitating disease that doctors said would leave him deaf for life. Two bones in his right ear had literally dissolved. The Sisters of the Blessed Sacrament told his parents to pray to Mother Katherine Drexel.

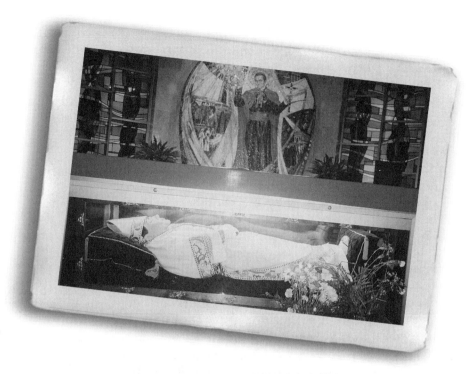

*The glass coffin containing the remains of Philadelphia's Bishop*
*John Neumann, America's first saint.*

That night in the hospital, fourteen-year-old Robert heard a
voice calling his name, heard it in his deaf ear. The next day
the amazed doctor found that his ear bones were regenerating
spontaneously. There was no medical explanation, although the
family knew the reason.

The second miracle attributed to Mother Katherine Drexel
also involved the deafness of a Bensalem child. Amy Wall was
one year old when she was diagnosed as incurably deaf. Her
parents, who had seen a TV show about the Gutherman miracle, obtained a piece of cloth from the habit worn by Mother
Katherine, placed it on the child's ear, and prayed. Four
months later, Amy Wall began hearing for the first time in her

life. When asked before the canonization of St. Katherine Drexel why she had been chosen for the miracle, the seven-year-old said, "Because God loves me and I love God."

The lives of Philadelphia's two saints could not have been more different in origin or more similar in purpose. The "Little Bishop," as Neumann was affectionately known (he stood five-foot-three), was born in Bohemia in 1811. He immigrated to America seeking to serve immigrant Catholics, and after being ordained a Redemptorist priest was assigned a parish on the frontier of Niagara, New York, where there were many German immigrants. Later he served as rector at St. Philomena's Church in Pittsburgh and St. Alphonsus in Baltimore before being consecrated Bishop of Philadelphia in 1852. As bishop he ministered to the Irish immigrants in coal country (he spoke Gaelic and seven other languages) and the Italian immigrants of South Philadelphia, establishing the first Italian parish, St. Mary Magdalene de Pazzi, after he purchased a former Methodist church. Neumann became an American citizen in 1848, and he established the first system of diocesan schools in his new country after he arrived in Philadelphia in 1852. On January 5, 1860, Bishop Neumann suffered a stroke while walking on the street not far from Philadelphia's new Cathedral of SS Peter and Paul on Logan Square. He died before last rites could be administered, but there is no doubt where his soul dwells.

Katherine Drexel was a socialite from one of the richest families in Philadelphia in the late 1800s. Her father, Francis Drexel, was a banker and business partner with J. P. Morgan. The Drexels were wealthy but charitable, and they opened their home three days a week to distribute food, clothing, and money to needy people. After entering the convent at the age of thirty, Katherine used her inheritance of $20 million to establish twelve schools for American Indians and more than one hundred rural and inner-city schools for black children. Among the thousands of children her religious order helped over the years was basketball legend Kareem Abdul-Jabbar, then a fourth-grader known as Lew Alcindor. He attended Holy Providence School in Bensalem in 1956 when it was called a mission school for "Indians and Colored People." The experience may have influenced Jabbar's later life, because in 2000 he wrote a book about his experiences as a volunteer high school basketball coach on the White Mountain Apache reservation in Arizona. You could say that Mother Drexel works in mysterious ways.

## ONE HUNDRED YEARS OF MUMMERY
### Philadelphia

The Mummers Parade on New Year's Day is Philadelphia and Pennsylvania's gift to the world. The gift comes wrapped in spangles and feathers and banjoes and saxophones and it takes the better part of ten hours to unwrap.

A cold-weather Mardi Gras—that's the best description I can come up with to describe the indescribable, a parade of 10,000 performers stretching for miles from South Philadelphia to Center City, strutting, marching, and cakewalking from dawn to dusk and into the night. It is a Philadelphia institution, a parade that comes but once a year and is the focus of thousands of families in neighborhoods around the city and suburbs for the entire year leading up to it.

So what's a Mummer? Fair question with a long answer, the end of which still doesn't answer the question adequately. Mummer is a word of German origin that means "disguise." The original Philadelphia Mummers didn't even call themselves mummers. They called themselves shooters, because it was their tradition from Colonial days to celebrate the new year by dressing up in costume and firing guns in the air. To this day the official name of the organization is the Philadelphia Mum-

# THE FROGS OF
# TWO STREET

James "Froggy" Carr was a tough little kid with an improbably deep voice (hence the nickname) from Second Street in South Philadelphia. The area is known affectionately as Two Street and is home to the majority of Mummers clubs, including the James "Froggy" Carr NYB (New Year's Brigade). The Frogs, as they are known, is an old-school comic club—all wenches all the time—that was formed by Froggy Carr's buddies after he died from a freak injury while playing a pickup game of tackle football in 1970. He was twenty years old at the time.

Froggy would have been fifty on New Year's Day 2001 and no doubt he would have been proud to see 650 boys and men dressed as wenches, chanting, "Who dat? Who dat? Who dat Froggy Carr?" as they marched up Market Street under the banner bearing his name. The Frogs, by far the largest single comic brigade in the Mummers Parade, are typical of the parade itself, something born in South Philadelphia that has taken on a life of its own. The 2001 parade was the fifth and final one under the leadership of Frogs Captain Mike Renzie.

The Frogs have marched in past parades as the Three Hundred Stooges (imagine a hundred Moes, a hundred Larrys, and a hundred Curleys all going "Wooo, wooo, wooo!" up Broad Street) and 300 Mickey Mouses (Mickey Mice?). As mice, they finished first for Mickey's fiftieth anniversary in 1989.

Despite their numbers and enthusiasm, the Frogs generally finish out of the money, if not actually in jail. One year Captain Mike Renzie ended up in police custody when

*The Frogs of Two Street frolic: Philadelphia Mummers strut in the new year wearing "wench" costumes in the comic division.*

the cops attempted to confiscate all the beer the Frogs had stockpiled in their support truck. Renzie protested, and was taken away. The Frogs responded by holding a sit-down strike in the middle of the parade route until their captain was returned, with lights flashing and sirens blasting. The entire parade came to a halt for forty-five minutes during the Frogs' sit down. This led to one of several disqualifications of the Froggy Carr brigade from the Mummers Parade over the years, but as the Frogs would tell you, they don't march for the prize money. They march because they're Mummers and it's Philadelphia and it's New Year's Day.

mers and Shooters Association, although guns have long since been holstered.

The ancient tradition of dressing up in eleborate costumes to celebrate the new year, or the return of the sun after the winter solstice, dates back to the Roman Saturnalia, when kings would dress as beggars and beggars would dress as kings. The whole concept of role reversal was key to the all-male (until the late 1970s) Mummer tradition: men dressed as women, called "wenches" in Mummerspeak. And until 1964, when the use of blackface was banned in the parade because of racial overtones, white men would dress as black men in fancy top hats and canes, calling themselves "dudes."

Dudes and wenches were the heart of the Comic Clubs, one of the four divisions in the Mummers Parade (comics, fancies, string bands, and fancy brigades). The parade today is far different from that first city-sponsored march "up the street" in 1901 to dedicate the new City Hall. For years the Mummers clubs would march informally up and down streets in "the Neck," the South Philadelphia neighborhoods situated on the neck of land between the Delaware and Schuylkill Rivers. The clubs would perform to the delight of spectators and homeowners who would voluntarily—and sometimes not so voluntarily—invite the well-armed Mummers into their houses for hot pepper pot soup or, better yet, hot cider or whiskey. Occassionally, well-lubricated Mummer clubs would confront each other while marching down the same street from opposite directions; these chance meetings frequently turned cranky rather than collegial. Alcohol and firearms have a way of mixing poorly.

In fact, it was the city's desire to control the violence on New Year's Day in South Philadelphia that led to the organized parade with the line of march uniformly north toward City Hall, where judging would be done and prizes awarded. To this day the intense rivalry between Mummers clubs is the competitive fuel that drives individual clubs to outdo each other each year, especially the string bands and fancy brigades, whose elaborate choreography, costumes, and musicianship rise to utterly more improbable levels of ingenuity and excellence every New Year's Day. In fact, that is the source of continuing friction among the Mummers. The comics contend that they are the heart of the parade, and they will march in any and all weather. The string bands and fancy brigades have hundreds of thousands of dollars invested in their eleborate satin and feathered "suits" and props, which will be ruined by rain or high winds. Thus, a number of parades have been postponed in the last twenty years, which has caused ill will among the already fractious Mummers clubs and the loyal fans who once lined Broad Street sidewalks six deep to watch the parade.

This led to the Market Street compromise. Rather than have a longer parade up sparsely populated Broad Street, the parade now begins at Fifth Street and progresses nine blocks up Market Street amid larger crowds of curbside spectators. At City Hall, marchers perform in front of the judges and the cameras and the millions watching the show on TV. The fancy brigades now perform their parade-finale routines indoors at the Pennsylvania Convention Center rather than risk the elements outdoors. Some Mummers, comics mostly, hate the new parade route, but it's the nature of Mummers to grumble while having the best time of their lives.

## THE PENNSYLVANIA X FILES
### *Philadelphia*

**W**hat Roswell, New Mexico, is to UFOs and what Bermuda is to mysterious triangles, Philadelphia is to disappearing warships. The so-called Philadelphia Experiment would definitely qualify as one of the X Files if Agents Mulder and Scully had decided to look into it. But it happened well before their time, during World War II, even though the story has yet to go away. As recently as November 28, 2000, the United States Navy's Office of Naval Research issued an updated statement on its "Frequently Asked Questions" page on the Internet addressing the Philadelphia Experiment. "Allegedly, in the fall of 1943, a U.S. Navy destroyer was made invisible and teleported from Philadelphia, Pennsylvania, to Norfolk, Virginia, in an incident known as the Philadelphia Experiment," began the Navy's earlier statement on September 2, 1996. "Records in the Operational Archives Branch of the Naval Historical Center have been repeatedly searched, but no documents have been located which confirm the event, or any interest by the Navy in attempting such an achievement."

I don't know about Agents Mulder and Scully, but such a denial makes a lot of people suspicious. When I logged on to the Philadelphia Experiment From A to Z home page on the Internet, I was visitor 327,605, indicating a continuing interest in the story, which first surfaced in the 1950s and was brought to prominence by a popular movie in the 1980s. The story, if not the facts, behind the Philadelphia Experiment is this:

In June of 1945 the USS *Eldridge,* a destroyer escort, was fitted with an experimental electromagnetic generation system at the Philadelphia Navy Ship Yard. The goal of the experiment was to make the ship invisible to radar. At 0900 hours on July 22, 1943, the *Eldridge* radar invisibility system was tested in front of naval observers. A greenish fog was said to have enveloped the ship, making it invisible to radar. Then the fog vanished along with the ship, which was no longer visible to the human eye either. After fifteen minutes, the order was given to shut down the electromagnetic field, and the *Eldridge* returned to view at anchor where it had been all along. Upon boarding the ship after the experiment, the naval observers found the crew members to be nauseated and disoriented.

The crew was replaced with a new crew, alterations were made to the electromagnetic equipment, and another test was conducted on the *Eldridge* at 1715 hours on October 28, 1943.

This time the ship vanished in a burst of intense blue light and reappeared hundreds of miles away at the Norfolk Navy Ship Yard, where it was observed by the crew of a civilian merchant ship, the SS *Andrew Furuseth*. Minutes later, the ship vanished from Norfolk and reappeared in Philadelphia. This time, when the observers boarded the *Eldridge,* they not only found crew members violently ill and out of their minds, but some sailors were missing altogether and five of the crew had been horribly fused to the metal of the ship's structure.

Or so the story goes. The truth is out there, as the *X Files* TV show likes to remind us. The Navy's latest statement on the Philadelphia Experiment offers transcripts of deck logs from both the *Eldridge* and the *Andrew Furuseth,* showing that the *Eldridge* was never in Philadelphia during the summer or fall of 1943 and that the *Andrew Furuseth* was not in Norfolk on October 28, 1943.

## WHAT KILLED THE DINOSAURS
### Philadelphia

The Tree House at the Philadelphia Zoo is designed for children—giant molded plastic insects crawling over a tropical rain forest—but there is plenty for keen-eyed adults to notice and enjoy. For instance, on one wall is a mural showing colorfully painted duck-billed dinosaurs tending their hatchlings. But if you walk up to the mother dinosaur and look into its one huge eye, you will see a reflection of perhaps the last things the dinosaurs saw before their extinction: the Golden Arches of McDonald's. And you thought it was an asteroid.

# THE SCHUYLKILL:
## A Spelling Bee of a River

*Most rivers in Pennsylvania have names of Indian origin: Susquehanna, Allegheny, Monongahela, Lehigh, Lackawanna. Even the Delaware, which is not an Indian name (it takes its name from the English Lord De La Warr), became the name commonly used to identify the Indian tribe known as Lenni Lenape.*

*The Schuylkill, however, is of Dutch origin (the word, not the river). There are many regular commuters on the Expressway that bears the river's name who will swear that the word* Schuylkill *in any language means "this lane ends suddenly." But in Dutch it means "hidden river," which, in fact, makes the term Schuylkill River as redundant as Rio Grande River.*

*The Schuylkill was named by Henry Hudson, the English explorer under Dutch hire who gave his name to a river in New York. During one of his explorations in the early 1600s, Hudson sailed up the Delaware River and passed without noticing the mouth of the Schuylkill, which was covered with reeds. On his way back down the Delaware, Hudson saw the mouth of the Schuylkill for what it was. He explored its navigable sections and gave it the name "hidden river."*

*As difficult as the Schuylkill was for Hudson to find, the name he gave the river has proved difficult for first-time visitors to pronounce and a continuing challenge for even lifelong Pennsylvanians to spell. There is a hard "C" sound at the beginning, not a soft "Sh": skoo-kill (although Philadelphians tend to pronounce it skook'll).* Schuylkill *is always a spelling bee champion breaker. Someone—certainly not Henry Hudson—came up with a mnemonic to help kids remember how to spell it: Seven Cooties Hurry Up Your Leg—Kick It Lots, Lee!*

# NOT YOUR AVERAGE CABBAGE GARDEN
## Philadelphia

Philadelphia's Fairmount Park has long held the title of
"world's largest urban park." In fact, when you look at a
map of Philadelphia, one of the most notable features is the
amount of green parkland in the heart of the city. This was no
accident, although the original motivation behind preserving
green space was to protect the city's water supply from industrial pollution. Today Fairmount Park is a system of land-
scaped and natural parkland totaling 8,000 acres, with fingers
of green touching dozens of neighborhoods. In fact, it is possible to walk from Philadelphia's City Hall in Center City to the
Montgomery County line 12 miles away without ever stepping
outside of Fairmount Park.

"Is it possible you have never seen Fairmount Park?" wrote
the well-traveled writer Lafcadio Hearn to a friend in New York
after a visit to the Centennial Exhibition in Philadelphia in
1876. "Believe me then it is the most beautiful place in the
whole civilized world. Your Central Park is a cabbage garden
by comparison." Such rave reviews for Fairmount Park were
exactly what the city leaders were counting on when they created the park in 1865. In fact, one of the assemblymen in the
two city councils governing the city in the mid-1800s urged
his fellow legislators to vote in favor of creating the park,
using the kind of language usually associated with ending
poverty or guaranteeing world peace. Said Assemblyman
James Miller in 1865, "We have it in our power, by saying aye
to this bill, to give Philadelphia as fair a landscape and as
charming a scene as ever gladened the eye of mortal man since
the gates of Eden were closed to human eyes—a place where
children may play, the young may ramble and the aged rest—a

place where philosophy may linger, art my revel, and beauty may find a perpetual home. Seldom in your lives will you have the opportunity of doing so much good by a single vote. . . . The blessings of childhood will follow you, the benediction of age will be upon you, and the generations to come will hold your name in grateful remembrance."

Most Philadelphians couldn't tell you who James Miller was, but certainly they are grateful for the park he and his fellow legislators gave the city.

# THE HIDDEN INDIAN

*In the heart of the Wissahickon Valley in Philadelphia's Fairmount Park, in the middle of a gorge where it's hard to imagine that you are surrounded by a city of a million and a half people, there is an outcropping of rock. And on that outcropping of rock crouches a 12-foot-tall Indian in full headdress. It is a limestone statue of the last of the chiefs of the Lenni Lenape, who inhabited the area in the 1700s. The actual chief, Teedyuscung, may or may not have resembled the noble warrior who peers out over the valley with his hand shading his eyes. But "finding the Indian" in Fairmount Park has become one of the traditions of parents and children since the statue was installed in its out-of-the-way location, accessible only by a dirt trail up steep terrain.*

*The statue of Teedyuscung originally stood in front of a tavern on Henry Avenue during the 1800s. It was moved to its current difficult-to-find location in 1910. It is one of the best-kept secrets of Fairmount Park and it can be found by intrepid explorers off Forbidden Drive (great name, huh?) near the stone bridge over the Wissahickon Creek at Rex Street. The fate of the original Teedyuscung is a sadder story. After taking his people to the Wyoming Valley in what is Luzerne County today, Teedyuscung died in a fire set by rival Iroquois tribe members in 1763.*

## CITY OF THE DEAD
### Philadelphia

P hiladelphia has its share of prominent and architecturally significant cemeteries, none more prominent and architecturally significant than Laurel Hill Cemetery on the edge of North Philadelphia. Overlooking the Schuylkill River, Laurel Hill's seventy-eight acres are laid out like a promenade for the living rather than a resting place for the dead. Designed by Scottish architect John Notman, upon opening in 1836 Laurel Hill immediately became a destination for city-bound Philadelphians seeking a rural retreat, a place to picnic and stroll among the marble monuments.

Located three and a half miles from Center City, Laurel Hill's landscaping set the tone for later development of Fairmount Park, which eventually spread to its very gates. Within the cemetery, which was declared a National Historical Landmark in 1998, are hundreds of exquisitely sculpted monuments, such as the tomb of William Warner, young son of William and Anna Catherine Warner, who died on January 20, 1889. The tomb shows a woman pulling aside the top of a stone sarcophagus, allowing a spirit, a face shrouded by wings, to soar to heaven. Over the years this striking work has been vandalized (both of the woman's arms are missing), but like a Venus de Milo of the Departed, her serenity is enhanced by the loss of her extremities.

On the back of the tomb is the monument maker's signature, "A. Calder, Philadelphia." That would be Alexander Milne Calder, the artist responsible for the huge bronze statue of William Penn and the other 250 pieces of statuary adorning City Hall. The date of young Warner's death reveals that Calder was in the middle of the forty-year-long project that was the design and construction of City Hall when he accepted the commission to sculpt this grave monument. As you can see, the artist did not treat this stunning work with any less attention than he devoted to the statues on City Hall.

Among the better-known Philadelphians buried in Laurel Hill Cemetery are Anna Jarvis, the founder of Mother's Day; George Meade, the victorious Union general at the Battle of Gettysburg; and Owen Wister, the author who wrote the first "western" novel, called *The Virginian*. Laurel Hill is open daily for tours.

*Armless woman raises the coffin lid to allow the soul of the departed to rise to heaven in a gravesite at Laurel Hill Cemetery in Philadelphia.*

## LOSING OLD BALDY
### *Philadelphia*

For some reason, General George Meade, the commanding officer of the victorious Union troops at the Battle of Gettysburg, gets short shrift from history, or at least from modern historians. In Ken Burns's PBS series *The Civil War*, Meade barely rates a mention compared to lesser Union commanders, and especially in comparison to Robert E. Lee. Perhaps it's because Meade was so plug ugly. With his bulging eyes and pinched mouth, Meade was nicknamed "old snapping turtle" by his troops. Now, even in Meade's hometown of Philadelphia, his memory is in danger of being further ignored because Old Baldy may have to find a new home.

Old Baldy, General Meade's horse, was wounded fourteen times in battle before being retired. Despite his war wounds, Old Baldy outlived Meade by ten years and was the riderless horse in Meade's funeral procession. When Old Baldy died in 1882, a couple of Civil War veterans dug up his body and had the horse's head mounted by a taxidermist. Old Baldy's noggin is now one of the most notable displays in the Civil War Library and Museum at 1805 Pine Street in Philadelphia. The museum, founded in 1888, is located in a town house around the corner from where Meade lived on Nineteenth Street near Rittenhouse Square. Because of financial difficulties, the Civil War Library and Museum's collections, including Old Baldy, may end up being sold to a Civil War Museum in Richmond, Virginia, making the Capital of the Confederacy his final resting place.

## IT'S NOT WEIRD, IT'S MUTTER
### *Philadelphia*

**W**henever I told friends and acquaintances from Philadelphia that I was working on a book called *Pennsylvania Curiosities*, almost immediately would come the comment, "You gotta have the Mutter Museum in there." Of course, the Mutter Museum is in here. If there were an encyclopedia listing for "Curiosities, Pennsylvania," it would include a little illustration of the Mutter Museum of the College of Physicians at 19 South 22nd Street, Philadelphia.

Where else could you see the cancerous tumor removed from the jaw of President Grover Cleveland during a secret operation aboard a private yacht in 1893? Where else could you find a body cast of the original Siamese twins, Chang and Eng Bunker, who underwent an autopsy at the College of Physicians after their death in 1874? Where else could you find the "soap lady," a victim of yellow fever in the 1800s whose corpse turned into a soaplike substance after being buried in alkaline soil?

What would become the Mutter Museum started with a collection of anatomical pathologies donated by Dr. Isaac Parrish in 1849. It was expanded by the larger collection donated by Dr. Thomas Dent Mutter in 1856, including bladder stones removed from Chief Justice John Marshall and the skeleton of a woman whose rib cage had been compressed by the habitual wearing of a tight corset. The collection now includes a mind-boggling number of medical abnormalities and antique medical instruments, including the first wooden stethoscope invented in 1816, Florence Nightingale's sewing kit, and a full-scale model of the first successful heart-lung machine designed by Philadelphia physician Dr. John H. Gibbon in 1953.

Although by laymen's standards, the Mutter Museum ranks high on the "Ewwwww!" meter, it is a serious museum of medical history. There is a display of 139 skulls from Eastern and

Central Europe as well as the skeleton of a man whose bones appear to have razor-sharp edges, causing him to live and die in almost unimaginably excruciating pain. And then there is the exhibit of the Mega Colon, a piece of large intestine that more closely resembles a giant caterpillar 27 feet long and 8 feet in circumference. It was removed from inside a man who failed to survive the operation.

Upon request, Gretchen Worden, Mutter Museum curator, has been known to display some of the museum's off-exhibit curiosities, including abnormalities of male genitalia. But don't tell her who told you.

## WHERE BAD IS AS GOOD AS IT GETS
### Philadelphia

Life under the El is as loud as the screech and rumble of a fast-moving train overhead. It is grim and terribly real to the thousands who live and work within sound and sight of this 17-block-long erector set of a railway over Market Street in West Philadelphia. There are too many criminals and not enough cops. Law and order is a lottery here, and 911 is the daily number.

But talk to the people on the 6100 block of Market Street— people like the beverage wholesaler who's been there since the early '60s, or the family who run the grocery store they bought a few years ago, or the widow of the saloonkeeper who still operates the bar the couple owned when Dick Clark was spinning records on *Bandstand* at WFIL studios under the same El just 15 blocks away—and they will tell you something strange.

These people will tell you that they feel safer on this one gloomy patch of Market Street, not because of the police, not because of politicians, not because of Town Watch. They feel safer because of their friendly neighborhood motorcycle gang, the Wheels of Soul.

"The Wheels is better than the police," says a young woman from the neighborhood, "because they's always there."

It's that simple. They're always there, just behind the door of their clubhouse, the black door with the white letters painted on it: DEATH TO THE KKK. And when there's trouble, the Wheels roll.

A few years ago, some young boys were trying to shake down some storeowners for a street tax, but the Wheels put a stop to it. A half dozen of them waited in the kitchen of the grocery, and when the punks arrived for their payoff, the Wheels emerged carrying baseball bats and other tax abaters. That was the last time the young boys attempted freelance block collections anywhere near the Wheels.

Another time, Philadelphia police officer Tyler Bullock of the 19th District stopped a car at 61st and Market, and the situation became hairy in a hurry. "I was involved with a confrontation with individuals in the car, and suddenly I turned around and there were these big guys from the Wheels of Soul standing behind me and asking me if I needed help. That evened up the odds."

More recently, trouble beneath the El came from heavily armed crack merchants who recruit young boys off the street to operate drug houses. They tried to operate a drug house on Dewey Street around the corner from the Wheels' clubhouse. The Wheels sent a delegation to greet them. No one mistook them for the Welcome Wagon.

"There were some gunshots," says one of the club's leaders, describing the negotiations. "Later on, there was a fire. There ain't no crack house on Dewey Street."

It's not uncommon for the phone at the Wheels of Soul clubhouse to ring with a request for an escort—to walk a woman to the bank so she can cash her check or maybe to walk an old man who's had too much to drink home from the local bar.

The Wheels are proud "one-percenters," a reference to the decades-old claim by the American Motorcycle Association that 99 percent of motorcycle riders are good, clean, upstanding citizens. The Wheels are self-described outlaws who live within the law, most of the time. They operate under their own Golden Rule: "You treat us good, we treat you better. You treat us bad, we'll show you how bad bad can be." You can work up a pretty impressive rap sheet showing how bad bad can be, and a number of Wheels have done time for weapons offenses and assault.

The Wheels have chapters in several states, and Philadelphia is their Mother Chapter. Mother has thirty members. Maybe fifty. Maybe more. Who knows? They won't say. Unlike many motorcycle clubs, the membership is multiracial. Blacks mostly, but there are whites, Chicanos, and Asians. The only overt prejudice is directed at Japanese motorcycles. Most of the active members are in their thirties and forties and hold down full-time jobs. Nevertheless, by middle-class standards, they are scary looking dudes, and proud of it. You can almost hear the clicking of door locks as cars pull up to the traffic light in front of the clubhouse.

And now the Wheels find themselves cast in the role of El's angels by their neighbors.

There is an exquisite irony in all this. There is a troublesome reality behind this motorcycle-club-with-a-heart-of-gold story. The reality is that the situation on the streets of West Philadelphia got so bad that these Harley homeboys emerged as peacekeepers by default, like a righteous outcropping of rock on a beach where the tide of evil has washed away the working-class sand. In neighborhoods ravaged by the crack pipe and abandoned by the law, there is a vacuum of authority. The Wheels have filled the vacuum simply because they are visible and they are willing to take a stand.

They're no Boy Scouts, but then, you don't find many merit badges awarded under the El.

# DIXIE STARTS HERE

Throughout history there have been pairings of names that have become instantly recognized—Lewis and Clark, Woodward and Bernstein, Sears and Roebuck, Seigfried and Roy—but no two Pennsylvania names have had a greater impact on the way America sees itself than Mason and Dixon.

The story of what brought Charles Mason and Jeremiah Dixon to Pennsylvania in 1763 begins with a dispute almost a century earlier between William Penn and Lord Baltimore. In 1682, when Pennsylvania's "proprietor" William Penn arrived in his newly granted colony, the Calverts, the founding family of Maryland, had been settled for exactly fifty years. Both the Calverts and the Penns had been granted land by kings of England (both kings, as luck would have it, were named Charles.) Charles I granted Lord Baltimore the province of Maryland in 1632. Charles I was separated from his crown, and subsequently his head, by Oliver Cromwell, and Charles II eventually assumed his father's throne in 1661. Maybe the records were lost along with the first Charles's head, but no sooner had the second Charles granted a charter to William Penn than the Calverts and Penns were yelping at each other over who owned what and where.

What would become the state of Delaware, for instance, was in dispute. Pennsylvania claimed "the lower three counties" as hers. Maryland said otherwise, and the people living in the three counties that compose the state of Delaware were already acting like an independent colony by the time two Englishmen, an astronomer and a surveyor by the names of Mason and Dixon, were sent over to clear up the mess.

The British courts had ruled that the east-west boundary line between Pennsylvania and Maryland should begin exactly 15 miles due south of Philadelphia, which Mr. Mason and Mr. Dixon soon discovered placed them in New Jersey, of all places. But they persevered, and four years later had completed the Mason-Dixon line, which included an arc representing the Pennsylvania–Delaware border, as well as a north-south line representing the Delaware–Maryland border. But the Mason-Dixon Line that became famous through American history as the demarcation line between north and south, free and slave, Union and Confederate, was the east-west line separating Pennsylvania and Maryland.

The literal Mason-Dixon Line runs for 233 miles along 39° 43' north latitude. It ends where Maryland meets West Virginia at the Pennsylvania border in Fayette County about five miles west of the Youghiogheny River Lake. The more symbolic Mason-Dixon line between north and south was created by the Missouri Compromise in 1820. The line extended from Pennsylvania's southern boundary west to where the Ohio River empties into the Mississippi and farther west along 36° 30' north latitude.

The Missouri Compromise separated America into free and slave states until the Civil War. By that time, the south was known to all, friend and foe, as Dixie. In fact, Dixie takes its name not from Jeremiah Dixon but from the nickname for French currency used in the big river port in New Orleans. "Dix" was French for "ten-spot." Dixie was also the name of a popular black character in a minstrel show from 1850; Dixieland was where he lived.

## *N o w* **T h a t ' s** *a* **C i t y** **H a l l !**
*P h i l a d e l p h i a*

There is a famous tower in Copenhagen, Denmark, built in the early 1900s and decorated with a mosaic depicting "The Eight Wonders of the Modern World." Included among them is Philadelphia's City Hall, a modern wonder that celebrated its one-hundredth birthday in 2001. City Hall stands at Philadelphia's ground zero, geographically, politically, and architecturally. It is literally the center of Center City, occupying four and a half acres where Broad Street would intersect Market Street. Like the middle of a compass, all Philadelphia directions—north, south, east, and west—use City Hall as their starting point.

Everything about City Hall is big. The 37-foot-tall bronze statue of William Penn on top of City Hall tower is the largest statue on a building in the world. The 548-foot-tall tower itself is the tallest masonry structure in the world. At the time of its construction, it was the largest municipal building in the country, literally twice the size of the U.S. Capitol. And the "time of its construction" was a period of almost forty years. Ground was broken in 1871 and the interior of the building wasn't finished until 1909, although the building was officially "presented" to the city in 1901 by the special Commission of the Erection of Public Buildings appointed by the state legislature.

You'll note that the name of the commission refers to Public "Buildings" not "Building." One of the first surprises citizens of Philadelphia experienced regarding City Hall was that it was one massive structure rather than four separate buildings occupying the intersection of Broad and Market. This led to City Hall being dubbed the "world's largest traffic obstruction" by countless millions of drivers, whether behind the wheel of a car or the reins of a horse and carriage in 1871.

Everything about City Hall is too much: 88 million bricks; enough marble, granite, and limestone to pave eighteen football fields; 250 individual pieces of statuary—the building simply overwhelms. When conceived, it was to be Philadelphia's statement about itself to the world, as overinflated as the building itself. Its architectural style, French Second Empire, had fallen out of style before the building was even completed. What was supposed to be a point of civic pride was seen as a civic embarrassment by many. In a nation falling in love with skyscrapers, City Hall was about as lean and mean-looking as a wedding cake. Whereas New York's skyline reached for the stars, Philadelphia's squatted on its haunches. For eighty-five years, no building in Philadelphia surpassed the top of City Hall tower (thirty-four stories) due to a charming "gentleman's agreement" known as the Billy Penn's Hat Rule.

Today there are several buildings in Center City taller than City Hall, its once dominant tower now a minor player in the city's skyline. Residual resentment toward City Hall as a symbol of Philadelphia stodginess has turned to affection. No one would dream of tearing City Hall down, as they once proposed in the early 1950s. (It was discovered that it would cost more to demolish the structure than it did to construct it.) They just don't *build* buildings like City Hall anymore. In 1957 the American Institute of Architecture declared City Hall to be "perhaps the greatest single effort of late nineteenth-century architecture." During the new millennium, City Hall is getting a face-lift that will take an estimated eight years and cost $125 million, which is about $100 million *more* than the cost of building it.

Free walking tours of City Hall are offered Monday through Friday at 12:30 P.M. Tours of the City Hall tower start every fifteen minutes from 9:30 A.M. to 4:30 P.M. Monday through Friday. The tour office is located in Room 121 of City Hall. Call 215–686–2840.

# WHY HE'S CALLED THE FOUNDING "FATHER"

One of Philadelphia's best-known "inside" jokes has to do with the statue of William Penn atop City Hall. The 37-foot-tall bronze statue shows the Quaker-hatted Penn standing with his left hand resting on a copy of Pennsylvania's Charter of Privileges spread out on top of a tree trunk. His right hand is turned downward and bent at the wrist slightly below his waist with his two-and-a-half-foot-long fingers pointing outward in the direction of Shackamaxon, the location on the Delaware River where Penn signed his famous treaty with the Indians under a spreading elm tree.

As luck or circumstance would have it, Shackamaxon is northeast of City Hall, which is the direction Penn is facing, which means that Penn's face is never in direct sunlight, which further means his outstretched hand is seen only in silhouette shaded from the sun by his body. When seen from the northwest, which happens to be the straight line down the Benjamin Franklin Parkway from the Art Museum, the outstretched fingers of William's Penn's hand seen in silhouette below his waist look more like his, well, let's put it this way—no wonder he's called Pennsylvania's Founding "Father."

The "dirty" angle of viewing William Penn has been the subject of both civic embarrassment and mirth, not to mention the topic of irreverent Philly T-shirt humor. It is the kind of detail proper Philadelphians pretend not to notice, although the desire to ignore the obvious can lead to ridiculous attempts to disguise it. For instance, in the fall of 1972, the Philadelphia Inquirer published a business magazine supplement featuring a prominent photo of William Penn atop City Hall on its cover. What was not prominent, in fact, what was missing altogether, was any sign of William Penn's offending hand, which had been airbrushed out of the photo.

## THE LIBERTY BELL: CRACKS, TYPOS, MISSING CHUNKS, AND ALL
### Philadelphia

I love the story of the Liberty Bell because, well, it's so totally American. It is a story of flaws overcome and scars worn proudly. It is a story of false starts and ingenious solutions. It is a story of misunderstandings and myths that make the simple truth all the more powerful.

For instance, the Liberty Bell never rang on July 4, 1776. And it was the Civil War, not the Revolutionary War, that brought the Liberty Bell to the attention of the world. And the famous "crack" most people recognize is actually a repair. And only a Pennsylvanian would probably notice or be chagrined by that fact that the word *Pennsylvania* is spelled wrong on the bell that countless millions have seen and touched.

First things first. The bell began life in 1751 when the Pennsylvania Assembly ordered a bell for the State House (now Independence Hall) in Philadelphia. The chairman of the assembly, Issac Norris, ordered the bell from Whitechapel Foundry in London, specifying in his instructions: "Let the Bell be cast by the best Workmen & examined carefully before it is Shipped with the following words well shaped in large letters . . . By order of the Assembly of the Province of Pensylvania for the State House in the city of Phila 1752." (Note the spelling of Pennsylvania in Norris's instructions.)

The bell arrived in Philadelphia in September 1752. The first time it was tested, Norris wrote, "I had the Mortification to hear that it was cracked by a stroke of the clapper without any other violence as it was hung up to try the sound." To the rescue came John Pass and John Stow, two Philadelphia foundry craftsmen, who agreed to recast the 2,081-pound bell

*Anyone notice which word is misspelled on the Liberty Bell?*

for a price of 36 British pounds, not to mention the immortality of having the names Pass and Stow forever emblazoned in large letters on the Liberty Bell.

Nobody had heard the sound of the original bell sent from England, so they had nothing to compare it to, but when the community verdict on the Pass and Stow bell was a resounding "HATED it!" The Assembly voted funds to purchase a new bell from London, but when it arrived in 1754, everyone but Pass and Stow was disappointed to discover that it sounded no better than the Philadelphia recast. The new bell from England was placed in the state house cupola to ring the hours, and the Pass and Stow bell remained in the State House steeple to ring on special occasions. (In 1772 neighbors passed around a petition complaining that they were "incommoded and distressed" by the constant "ringing of the great Bell in the steeple" of the State House.)

The bell never rang on July 4, 1776, because the Declaration of Independence was at the printers being reproduced. It summoned Philadelphians to the first public reading of the Declaration in the State House Courtyard on July 8, 1776. A year later the bell was removed from Philadelphia along with all the other bells in town to prevent the invading British troops from melting them down into cannonballs or Wilkinson sword blades.

After the Revolutionary War, the bell returned to the State House, where it rang on special occasions such as the deaths of Presidents Washington, Adams, and Jefferson, and Supreme Court Justice John Marshall. No one agrees on when the new crack first appeared, except that it was discovered before 1846 and that a repair job was attempted by drilling out the existing hairline crack so that the sides of the bell wouldn't rub together and cause a buzzing sound when rung. On February 14, 1846, while tolling for Washington's birthday, the buzz returned, along with the discovery of a new hairline crack. That was the end of the bell's ringing days, but only the beginning of its story.

Even before the crack became famous, the bell was adopted by the antislavery movement because of the Biblical inscription from Leviticus around the top of the bell: PROCLAIM LIBERTY THROUGHOUT ALL THE LAND AND UNTO ALL THE INHABITANTS THEREOF. To the abolitionists, the operative word in that passage was "all" as much as "Liberty." The first use of the term Liberty Bell is dated 1839 in a poem about the bell in the antislavery publication *Liberator*.

The Civil War cemented the reputation of the Liberty Bell as a symbol for a fractured nation seeking to heal itself. After being put on display during the 1876 Centennial Celebration in Philadelphia, the Liberty Bell toured the country several times. New Orleans, Chicago, Charleston, Boston, St. Louis, and San Francisco all hosted the bell during celebrations between 1885 and 1915. In those thirty years, souvenir hunters had managed to chisel and chip away thirty pounds of metal from the bell mouth's (you can see for yourself). After that, the city of Philadelphia, which owns the bell, passed legislation forbidding the bell from ever leaving the city again. And it never has. (The Liberty Bell, enclosed in glass, can be seen daily from 9:00 A.M. to 5:00 P.M. at the Liberty Bell Pavilion between Fifth and Sixth on Market Street. Admission is free.)

## THINKING ABOUT THE RODIN MUSEUM
### Philadelphia

The Gates of Hell hang in Philadelphia and The Thinker sits before them, pondering, perhaps, the choices one faces in life. These sculptures by the great French artist Auguste Rodin reside in a tiny but impressive museum on the Benjamin Franklin Parkway, Philadelphia's gateway boulevard modeled after the Champs Élysées. The gardened gateway to the Rodin Museum itself is modeled after the facade of the Chateau d'Issy, which Rodin had moved to his studio in Meudon, France. Inside the museum are 125 sculptures completed by Rodin, the largest collection of his work outside Paris.

For this jewel box of a museum we have a movie-palace magnate to thank. Jules E. Mastbaum was a Philadelphia movie theater mogul back in the days when red carpets and velvet curtains and white-gloved ticket takers greeted arriving moviegoers, back in the days when movies were an event rather than a couple of hours kill at the mall multiplex. You could fit a half dozen Rodin Museums into one of Mastbaum's movie theaters back in the 1920s when Jules Mastbaum began collecting the works of the artist, who died at the age of seventy-seven in 1917. Among those works is *The Thinker,* perhaps the most famous statue in the world. Philadelphia's 800-pound bronze is one of seventeen casts made of the original. Mastbaum commissioned the museum housing Rodin's works to complement the massive Philadelphia Museum of Art a few blocks away. Among the masterpieces in the Rodin Museum are *The Burghers of Calais, Eternal Springtime,* and Rodin's epic bronze doors, *The Gates of Hell,* which the artist worked on for thirty-seven years.

## MARIO LANZA AND THE CORNER BOY CULT
### Philadelphia

Back in the mid-1970s, actor Tony Randall starred in a TV sitcom called *The Tony Randall Show* in which he played a Philadelphia Common Pleas Court judge. In the first episode, he meets his new administrative assistant named Mario Lanza. "Are you related?' asks Randall. "To who?" asks the assistant. "Mario Lanza," says the judge. "I am Mario Lanza," comes the reply, without a trace of self-consciousness. Mario is, after all, as common a name in South Philadelphia as Todd and Ashley are in the suburbs. Ironically, the most famous Philadelphia Mario wasn't a Mario at all. Alfredo Cacozza was Mario Lanza's given name. His friends called him Freddy.

*At the Mario Lanza Museum in Philadelphia, framed*

*newspaper headlines report his death in 1959.*

Freddy Cacozza was a barrel-chested South Philly corner boy who was as good with his fists as he was with his voice. He was encouraged to leave South Philadelphia High School because of fighting, and his only class picture from that period was during his days at Vare Junior High School in South Philadelphia. He is seen standing in the back row just a few students away from another famous Philadelphian also good with his fists, future Mayor Frank Rizzo. You can see that class picture and other artifacts from the career of Freddy Cacozza at the Mario Lanza Museum located in the Settlement Music School at Fourth and Queen Streets in South Philadelphia. Mario Lanza (his mother's maiden name was Maria Lanza), one of the greatest American tenors ever to sing on records and film, became a James Dean–type cult figure among opera buffs after his death at the age of thirty-eight. By then, Lanza's career in Hollywood as a movie matinee idol was already in a downward spiral. Lanza had an operatic temperament, and he made enemies.

But in Philadelphia where he grew up, he is remembered as one of the guys. Friends started the Mario Lanza Institute in his honor forty years ago. A museum featuring his clothes and recordings and gold records started in the back of a record store on Snyder Avenue and a few years ago moved to the Settlement Music School, not far from where Lanza grew up on the 600 block of Christian Street. The handsome young corner boy with the voice of an angel was discoverd by Hollywood after World War II. His first movie, *That Midnight Kiss,* with Kathryn Grayson and Ethel Barrymore, made its world premiere in Philadelphia in 1949. In *That Midnight Kiss* Lanza played a truck driver from Philadelphia who dreamed of being an opera star. In his next movie he played a fisherman who dreamed of being an opera star. In his next movie he was an opera star who dreamed of making a comeback. His last movie was *The Student Prince;* the white military uniform he wore in that role is on display in the museum. Lanza died in Rome in 1959 in the midst of a European comeback attempt. (Mario Lanza Museum, 416 Queen Street, 3rd floor. Call 215–468–3623.)

## THEY'RE CALLED HOAGIES, AREN'T THEY?
### *Philadelphia*

E veryone knows that hoagies come from Philadelphia, right? But why? Why hoagie? And why have Philadelphia hoagies taken on a mystique of sorts that is absent from similar sandwiches in other cities? Elsewhere, these sandwiches are called heroes, subs, torpedoes, blimps, and—only in and around Norristown, Pennsylvania for some reason—zeps. Certainly those names are more descriptive of the general shape of hoagies, long Italian rolls cut lengthwise and filled to overflowing with meats, cheeses, and veggies. They *do* resemble submarines, torpedoes, blimps, and zeppelins, not to mention that they require a heroic appetite to finish.

But for some reason the mythology of hoagies has spread throughout the land, especially in the last ten years or so. You began to see and hear the word *hoagie* in places you never saw or heard it before—in *New Yorker* magazine cartoons and David Letterman monologues—key indications that hoagies have become hip. Now hoagies are mainstream American junk food, like Buffalo wings and Philadelphia cheese steaks.

But the word *hoagie*. Where did it come from? What follows is the more-or-less official version: During the First World War, Philadelphia's already booming shipbuilding industry went into overdrive. The shipyards provided ample work for skilled and unskilled Italian immigrants who arrived in Philadelphia in great numbers around the turn of the century. In 1890 there were 6,799 Italian-born citizens in Philadelphia; by 1920 there were 63,223, the vast majority of whom settled in South Philadelphia, not far from the city's largest private shipyard on Hog Island in the Delaware River.

The workmen at Hog Island were called Hoggies. An Italian Hoggie would typically carry his lunch in an oil-stained paper bag that contained an Italian roll sliced in half, slathered with olive oil on each side, and filled with cheese, tomatoes, lettuce, onions, peppers, and, if he was lucky, slices of salami. Imagine the aroma wafting around the workplace or a crowded streetcar from one of those sandwiches. Imagine someone saying, "I gotta get one of those sandwiches those Hoggies eat." So it doesn't take much imagination to see how the new sandwich sensation became known as a hoggie. How one of the *g*s became an *a* is anyone's guess. And how the "hah" sound morphed into the "ho" sound is a question for linguists to argue (although if it were up to marketing analysts the answer would be, "Don't you think 'hoggie' sounds entirely too *piggy?*").

So Philadelphia, exclusively, enjoyed its hoagies by that name for the better part the century, always certain of the hoagie's superiority over the less enigmatically named subs, the blimps, torpedoes, and heroes enjoyed by other cities. But sometime around 1990, the same way people in other cities started saying "Yo!" after all the *Rocky* movies, the word *hoagie* was embraced by people who wouldn't know Hog Island from Hoagy Carmichael.

One problem Philadelphians have with the success of hoagies as an export is with the rampant corruption of the "meaning" of the word *hoagie*. A hoagie can contain any number of meats, except chicken. A hoagie can be doctored to taste with any condiment, except mustard (for a long time, mayonnaise was the line, but that battle is long past). And a hoagie can be served cold from a refrigerator or, better, at room temperature. But never from an oven. A hoagie baked in an oven is called a grinder.

And a hoagie can never be what I found on an Internet Web site from Bedford, Indiana, under the heading HOAGIE RECIPE: "In a large bowl mix together Velveeta, chipped ham, sliced eggs, diced onion, diced pickles, and chopped olives. In small bowl mix together mayonnaise and chili sauce. Add small bowl mixture to large bowl mixture and mix. Put mixture on buns of your choice and wrap each one in foil. Refrigerate until almost ready to serve. Heat in 450-degree oven for 15–20 minutes. Makes approximately 16 hoagies if you use hot dog buns."

Whatever *that* is, it's not a hoagie. And whatever a hoagie is, it had to be invented in Philadelphia. Or Norristown—after all, *zep* is a great name for a hoagie.

## THE "INVENTION" OF THE PHILLY
## CHEESE STEAK
### Philadelphia

U nlike the hoagie, the origin of Philadelphia's other five-
star contribution to the American junk food pantheon,
the cheese steak (or for the lactose intolerant, the steak sandwich), is pretty much accepted as gospel. Like the fried baloney
sandwich, the steak sandwich just sort of *happened*. But unlike
fried baloney, the Philadelphia steak sandwich became a
national gastronomic, not to mention marketing, phenomenon.

It was during the dark days of the Great Depression (don't
all inspirational American success stories start out that way?)
when Pasquale "Pat" Olivieri, the son of Italian immigrants
who was born in South Philadelphia in 1907, was having a par-
ticularly bad day behind the counter of his hot dog stand at
Ninth and Wharton Streets. No business, no prospects, and
worst of all, Pat Oliveiri was sick of eating hot dogs. So he
splurged. "Get me some beefsteak," he said to his cousin, flip-
ping him a dime to buy a chunk-a chunk-a burnin' love from
the local butcher. Pat sliced the beefsteak into thin slices,
tossed it into a skillet on top of some sizzling oil, and cooked
himself a nice sandwich, which he was about to eat when—
behold—a customer poked his head over the counter and asked,
"What's that GREAT SMELL? I want whatever that is."

Pat Olivieri, hungry no doubt, was not a dope. He sold the
sandwich out of his hand, the proverbial shirt off his back. And
so a unique food industry was born. "Pat's King of Steaks"
became a family dynasty that continues today. The original
Pat's is still on the southwest corner of the triangle formed by
Ninth Street, Wharton Street, and Passyunk Avenue, the "fer-
tile crescent" if you will, of the cheese steak culture. You can

*It's four a.m. in South Philadelphia, time for a cheese steak.*

see a bronze plaque in the sidewalk outside the counter at Pat's, where Rocky Balboa stood dripping sauce on his shoes in the old original *Rocky* movie.

Pat's became a twenty-four-hour-a-day operation, an all-night diner open to the elements, but customers didn't care. There was something about freezing one's buns off while waiting for a sizzling cheese steak at three in the morning. People stood in line (still do, in fact) meekly waiting for the counterman to shout, "Next," at which time a customer had 2.7 seconds to give an order or be ordered to the end of the line. (And you thought the soup Nazi on *Seinfeld* was bad!). "Gimme a cheese with" means a cheese steak with fried onions. "Two cheese without" means two cheese steaks without fried onions. And woe be the person who asks the question, "What's with?" At that the counterman says, "Hey, fellas, we got one." All the kitchen crew put down their spatulas, crowd their faces into the two by two-and-a-half-foot window and shout, "With onions! STOOPID!" You don't want to be standing at the front of the line when that happens.

## *STEAK WARS: MAY THE CHEESE BE WITH YOU*

*In 1966 something unbelievable happened to Pat's cheese steak kingdom. A rival steak sandwich shop opened on the southeast corner of Ninth and Passyunk, catty-corner to Pat's Steaks, calling itself Geno's. In the thirty-some years since, the Great Steak Wars of Philadelphia have continued 24/7. The only days Geno's or Pat's is closed are Christmas and Easter. The war reached a peak in the mid-1980s when Geno's owner Joe Vento hung a banner across Ninth Street that said, Geno's. The freshest meats, cheeses, and breads. Also clean! You didn't have to read too deeply between the lines to understand who that last part was aimed at.*

*Throughout the Great Steak Wars, local politicians have wooed customers of each steak shop without declaring their personal preference. In one of the most brilliant diplomatic moves of his career, President Bill Clinton held a reelection rally in the middle of the intersection between the two steak shops in 1996. After the rally, Clinton and Mayor Ed Rendell walked to Pat's and ate a cheese steak. When they finished they marched over to Geno's and ate a cheese steak there. Then the President of the most powerful nation on earth told the assembled thousands that he couldn't choose which steak was better because they were both so good. That Clinton could charm the stripes off a zebra.*

## PHILADELPHIA SKY WALKERS
*Philadelphia*

T here is no written record of the first time children in
Philadelphia tied the shoelaces on a pair of sneakers
together and then flung them over telephone wires, but
chances are the first sneakers hanging from telephone wires
were sighted within days of the telephone conversation that
started with the words, "Mr. Watson, come here. I want you."

I threw sneakers up on the wire as a kid, and so did my
friends. It was a way of retiring a well-worn pair of Keds or Converse All-Stars, sort of like a Viking funeral in the sky. All who
looked upward would know that these shoes served someone well.

The custom of tossing sneakers over telephone wires almost
disappeared in Philadelphia during the 1980s, a period that coin-
cided with the rising popularity of footwear that required a second mortgage to purchase. The price tag on a pair of "sneaks"
increased in direct proportion to multimillion-dollar endorsement
contracts offered to athletes by Nike, Puma, and Adidas. No one
was tossing a pair of hundred-dollar energy-transfer cross-train-
ers over any stupid telephone wires. But with the prosperity of
the 1990s, the sneakers returned overhead, along with hiking
boots and any other footwear equipped with laces.

Nowhere in Philadelphia is the concentration of dangling
sky walkers more plentiful than the intersection of Eighth
Street and Lehigh Avenue in North Philadelphia (see photo).
Hundreds of pairs of all shapes and sizes and brand names
hang from these utility wires less than a block away from a
public middle school. The sneakers usually remain until the
laces rot from exposure or until city Streets Department crews
remove them because the accumulated weight poses a hazard.

*Sneakers hanging from the wires. A Philadelphia tradition continues at 8th and Lehigh in North Philly.*

## THE COWBOY
## IN THE REARVIEW MIRROR
### Philadelphia

rederic Remington was one of the most famous sculptors and illustrators in the late nineteenth and early twentieth centuries. It was Remington, on assignment to Cuba to illustrate Spanish atrocities and Cuban rebels before the outbreak of the Spanish-American War, who cabled the complaint to newspaper magnate William Randolph Hearst that there were no atrocities, there was no war. "You provide the pictures," Hearst cabled back. "I'll provide the war." Which he dutifully did.

Remington was most famous for his artwork depicting the American West. His illustrations and sculptures of the drama of western landscapes and native inhabitants, and his sculptures of ranch hands and sodbusters are classic American art icons. But the only life-size statue Remington ever completed stands on an outcropping of rock along Kelly Drive in Fairmount Park. The bronze, called simply *The Cowboy*, shows a rider pulling hard on the reins of his horse on the edge of a precipice. The horse's tail stands straight out from behind as an indication of fast motion or, perhaps, a stiff head wind.

The Cowboy, *overlooking Kelly Drive in Philadelphia, is*
*Frederic Remington's only life-size sculpture.*

Remington himself chose the exact site for the sculpture to stand, overlooking a slight bend in the road immediately below. When Remington chose the site, however, the river drives were cinder-covered horse-and-buggy thoroughfares where the fastest traffic traveled at 10 miles an hour. Now the speed limit is 40 mph and Kelly Drive is a busy and heavily traveled commuter route. Because there is no place to pull over on Kelly Drive to admire the statue, most motorists only see it as a blur flashing past on their way to and from work.

### THE "LEGENDARY" BLUE HORIZON
#### *Philadelphia*

Walk to the top of the stairs of a certain 135-year-old Victorian brownstone building on Broad Street in North Philadelphia and then turn right. As countless thousands before you have said upon seeing the boxing ring set up in the middle of the Blue Horizon auditorium, with its dark wooden balconies hanging almost over the ring ropes, you may mutter in awe, "This is like something out of a movie."

Yes it is. That's why fight fans everywhere, without self-inflated bravado, call it the "legendary Blue Horizon." This is the boxing venue hometown fighters dream of: a bout at the Blue, with friends, neighbors, and family cheering their lungs out. This is the inspiration for the Rocky Balboa type of club fighter from Philadelphia, the hometown boy who makes it big. When Philly boxer and USBA heavyweight champion Tim Witherspoon defended his title at the Blue in 1991, the description on the fight card began, "'Terrible Tim' Witherspoon, who has boxed in London's Wembley Stadium, the Omni in Atlanta, the Dunes Hotel in Las Vegas, the Sky Dome in Seattle, and Madison Square Garden, finally hits the big time tonight with his first ever Blue Horizon appearance in a scheduled twelve-round fight with Art Tucker." If that description was tongue-in-cheek, you couldn't see it for the mouthpiece.

The Blue Horizon is one of the most intimate and atmospheric fight venues in America, seating 1,200 people in an auditorium that has seen twenty-seven world champions box there at some point during their careers. The USA Network cemented the reputation of the "legendary Blue Horizon" by telecasting live *Tuesday Night Fights* from the Blue starting in 1987. ESPN2 added the Blue to its *Friday Night Fight* venues in 1998. The ancient facility has been struggling to meet modern zoning and fire code demands in recent years, and its future is uncertain. But it is a must-see for serious fight fans, even if they are only serious about watching the showgirls march around the ring with the round cards.

### FOOT 'N' MOUTH, TOOTH 'N' NAIL
*Philadelphia*

Philadelphia has a long history of medical accomplishments, including the first hospital in the United States, Pennsylvania Hospital at Ninth and Pine Streets. But among its lesser-known medical curiosities is the Shoe Museum at the Pennsylvania College of Podiatric Medicine at Sixth and Race Streets and the Dental Museum at the Temple University Dental School at Broad Street and Allegheny Avenue.

They aren't museums so much as displays. At the former you will find celebrity footwear, such as Julius Erving's autographed Dr. J's Converse basketball shoe, plus a gaudy collection of multicolor shoes worn by Ringo Starr. There are tiny shoes worn by ballerinas and enormous shoes worn by female giants. There are dress shoes worn by First Ladies Mamie Eisenhower, Betty Ford, and Nancy Reagan, as well as boxer's shoes worn by heavyweight champ Joe Frazier and one of Flyers goalie Bernie Parent's ice skates. One display case labeled THE FOOLISH FOOT shows ridiculously tall high-heeled shoes once believed to be fashionable. Another display case shows ethnic footwear, such as the teeny-tiny shoes worn by women with bound feet in pre-Communist China.

The Dental Museum contains more historically significant items, such as the first dental chair, dating from 1790, plus a number of Civil War–era dental kits, foot-powered drills, and early X-ray machines. One invention from the 1890s was an electric battery used to zap patients to increase their threshold of pain during root canal. Then there is the display devoted to the sixty-year career of one of America's most flamboyant and self-promoting dentists, Edgar "Painless" Packer. Packer plucked tens of thousands of teeth from the mouths of patients, most of which he saved. There's a display of a tooth necklace Packer made, plus a wooden bucket containing thousands of extracted teeth Packer pulled "painlessly" during his career.

## ROCK AND ROLL RINGING ROCKS
### Upper Black Eddy

Pennsylvania has a number of fields where boulders were deposited by retreating glaciers during the last Ice Age. Perhaps the most famous is Boulder Field in Hickory Run State Park in Carbon County, where boulders as round as cantaloupes and as big as Volkswagens are piled on top of one another in an eerie landscape surrounded by trees. But there's only one field where you can play rock and roll on the rolling rocks.

Ringing Rocks Park near Upper Black Eddy in Bucks County has been a place of mystery since the original inhabitants noticed that the boulders strewn about the field rang like bells when struck with a tomahawk. The same effect can be produced with a ball-peen hammer these days, and more than one musical group has traveled to the Ringing Rocks in an attempt to create the ultimate rock music. The first rock concert in the field was conducted by Dr. J. J. Ott, who led a group of musicians playing more traditional instruments in a performance for the Buckwampum Society of Bucks County in 1890. Dr. Ott played lead boulder in the concert. A witness at the time reported "the clear bell-like tone he was playing could be heard above the horns."

Over the years the theories as to why the Ringing Rocks ring have ranged from Native American spirits to UFOs to glaciers. One thing we know is that the Ringing Rocks are not a glacial deposit. They were the result of erosion, perhaps from an ancient riverbed. Within the past thirty years, the mystery of what makes these boulders ring has been explained by geologists as the result of molten magma cooling, placing the unique deposits of hard dark diabase minerals within under enormous stress. The effect of this stress was like tightening a guitar string. The rocks in the center of the field away from trees and under direct sunlight ring better than the rocks along the perimeter. Some people believe that the ringing rocks are the result of some bizarre magnetic energy field, which causes compasses to spin wildly and camera film negatives to be cloudy when developed. Scientific tests have revealed no unusual energy emissions from the area, which of course hasn't stopped anyone from claiming that weird things keep happening there. Back in 1987, during the so-called Harmonic Convergence, a group of new age believers gathered around the Ringing Rocks to chant "Om." The rocks did not chant back. (Call 215–757–0571. The park is located 2 miles west of Upper Black Eddy.)

## FORGET ARMY-NAVY
### Villanova

The last time a college from Pennsylvania won the NCAA Division I men's basketball championship was in 1985 when underdog Villanova played David to Georgetown's Goliath, and the defending national champion Hoyas fell under the 90 percent second-half field goal average of the overachieving Wildcats. It was also the last time that three teams out of the Final Four were Catholic universities. This caused a fair amount of intramural wagering among the members of the various religious orders that founded the three colleges represented. There were the Augustinians (O.S.A.) of Villanova, the Jesuits (S.J.) of St. Johns in New York, and the Vincentians (C.M.) of Georgetown. The rivalry among Catholic colleges is not unlike that of the United States military academies: They all play for the same commander in chief, but each branch of the service insists that its team is the best.

A joke making the rounds at the time went like this: Before the Final Four, the various heads of the three religious orders wrote a joint letter to God asking which teaching order of priests was the best. God replied in a letter that He couldn't possibly choose from among three such worthy religious orders and that he had no personal favorites. At the bottom of the letter was His signature, "God, S.J."

As it turned out, that year the Jesuits of St. Johns had to settle for a third place finish behind the Augustinians and the Vincentians. Incidentally, the only other Pennsylvania university to win the men's NCAA basketball championship was also a Philadelphia Catholic school—LaSalle in 1954, founded by the Christian Brothers (F.S.C.).

## A *MISH* R *OBOTS?*
### *Weaverton*

There's something creepy about the Weaverton One-Room Schoolhouse on Route 340 between Intercourse and Bird-in-Hand in Lancaster County. It's one of those un-Amish Amish attractions that dot the landscape of southeastern Pennsylvania. Somehow seeing Amish children depicted by robots seems to be the antithesis of the technological simplicity that orders Amish life.

The Weaverton One-Room Schoolhouse is a bright yellow one-story wooden structure that functioned as an actual schoolhouse for Amish youngsters from 1877 until 1969. The interior looks the way it would have in the 1930s, with blackboards lining the walls and desks lined up in neat rows. There's a potbellied stove in the back of the room that served as the sole source of heat as well as the lunch warmer. Baked potatoes sit on the stove as they did when Amish children attended school here and brought a potato from home for lunch.

The "animated scholars" or robot Amish kids that are activated during the shows are actually mannequins equipped with a couple of low-tech movements, such as raising a hand or dipping a girl's pigtails in an inkwell. The movements are part of a fifteen-minute presentation that includes a narrated history of the one-room school in the state of Pennsylvania. There was one teacher for as many as thirty students in grades one through eight. The lessons would range from learning the alphabet to long division and geography. Undoubtedly, the younger kids learned advanced material by osmosis and the older children in need of remedial education were exposed to the lessons taught to younger students. There were 396 such schools at one time serving Amish children. Shows run continuously from 10:00 A.M. until 5:00 P.M. from Easter through Thanksgiving.

*CAUTION: HORSE AND BUGGY AHEAD is a commonly seen traffic sign in Amish Country.*

## WHEN THE REBELS TOOK YORK
### York

York, Pennsylvania, holds the distinction of being the only capital of the United States ever to fall to Confederate troops during the Civil War. Of course, York wasn't the capital of the United States at the time, nor had it been for almost one hundred years. But York was technically the capital of the United States in 1777, after Congress had fled Philadelphia when British troops occupied the city during the Revolutionary

War. It was in York that the Articles of Confederation, America's first constitution, were adopted by Congress.

On June 26, 1863, Confederate General Jubal Early and 9,000 troops marched into York and occupied the town without a battle. The Stars and Stripes were hauled down from the flagpole in the town square and replaced with the Confederate battle flag. York was the largest northern city ever to fall to Robert E. Lee's invading Army of the Potomac. The Confederate occupation of York lasted four days. As the historical display in the York tourist center notes, on June 30, 1863, "Like many future visitors, Jubal Early and men traveled on to Gettysburg."

## THE HOUSE THAT HOFFMAN BUILT
### York

**B**ob Hoffman was a man's man and proud of it. Only a man's man would have the confidence to have a nearly nude larger-than-life-size bronze statue of himself cast and placed along a busy highway outside his place of business. You can see Bob Hoffman in bronze, next to Interstate 83 outside York. The statue stands in front of the Weightlifting Hall of Fame next to the York Barbell Company, which Hoffman founded. Hoffman was already an old man when he posed for the statue, but he still looked strong enough to lift an Oldsmobile.

Inside the Weightlifting Hall of Fame are artifacts from the era known as a "Strongmanism," when weight lifting was the stuff of carnivals and vaudeville acts. There's the 220-pound dumbbell used by nineteenth-century strongman Louis Cyrl, who lifted it easily over his head with one hand. Then there's the gaudy belt presented by *The National Police Gazette* to Warren Lincoln Travis for being the World's Strongest Man in

*Mural of Bob Hoffman, muscleman extrodinaire and York,*
*Pennsylvania, entrepeneur.*

1906. There are photos showing feats (and feets) of strength,
such as a strong man on his back supporting a bench holding
sixteen men on the bottom of his feet.

The Bob Hoffman Story (1898–1985) is told in another
room, showing young Hoffman after he returned to York following World War I. He founded the York Oil Burner Company,
the precursor to York Barbell Company. Hoffman organized a
weight lifting club among his employees that soon developed
into a national weight lifting organization. The first weight
lifting championships in America were held in York, which
soon became known as Muscletown, USA. Hoffman turned his
attention to full-time physical fitness in 1932 when he purchased *Strength and Health* magazine (there's a photo of four
men lifting Hoffman and another man in an automobile in

front of the publishing company offices). By the time he died at the age of eighty-seven, Hoffman was recognized as The Father of World Weightlifting and the company he founded as "the strongest name in fitness."

Alongside the Weightlifting Hall of Fame is the Body Building Hall of Fame, which is not about how much you can lift as much as how muscular you can become. Big difference. The heroes, of course, in the Body Building Hall of Fame are the original Mr. America, Steve Reeves, star of many badly dubbed Hercules movies in the '50s and '60s; and Mr. Universe, Arnold Schwarzenegger, who, as the caption next to his photo noted, "has had several movie roles since his retirement from competition." There's a photo of Schwarzenegger on the cover of a 1970 body building magazine where he is identified as "Arnold Strong, movie and TV star."

## THE HARLEY FACTORY TOUR: NO TIES REQUIRED
### York

Y ou're not allowed to bring a camera with you when you take the guided tour of the Harley-Davidson Final Assembly Plant off Route 30 in York. It may have something to do with industrial secrets, but most likely it's a safety measure. The last thing they need at the Harley assembly plant is some wide-eyed biker enthusiast with a camera stepping in front of a forklift speeding around the one-million-square-foot plant. And let me tell you, this tour is for real.

The first thing you have to do is turn over your camera to the tour guide, who locks it up for safekeeping. In exchange you'll receive a pair of plastic safety glasses and a radio receiver with an earpiece. The need for this soon becomes apparent because this is a working factory and working factories are loud. (I said, WORKING FACTORIES ARE LOUD!) Carl was the tour guide for my group of about twenty people, some who had come from as far away as Germany to see the inside of an American motorcycle factory. Carl is a retired schoolteacher, and as he led us onto the factory floor from the visitor center, we could hear his heavy breathing in our earpieces. Just when members of the tour were beginning to make amused eye contact about what we were hearing, Carl announced into his headset, "If you hear me breathing it's because I have asthma. If you don't hear me breathing, call 911."

As I said, this is a working factory, and the first thing Carl tells us is to stay inside the yellow lines painted on the floor so that we don't wander into the path of forklifts and carts moving heavy equipment from one end of the factory to the other. "That motorcycle you see there," says Carl, pointing to a finished product coming off the end of the assembly line, "was ordered by a customer more than a year ago." Harley's success in recent years has been a combination of a first-rate product meeting incredible customer loyalty and patience. Harley owners are a breed unto themselves. Not only are they willing to wait more than a year for the Harley of their choice, but they seem to rejoice in the process. And so do the Harley employees, a remarkably stable workforce with a turnover of only one percent a year in a factory employing 3,000 men and women. "And that one percent is people retiring," says Carl.

"You see anyone wearing a tie here?" Carl asks, as the tour group pauses in front of the testing area, where the finished product is taken off the assembly line and run through the gears up to 70 miles per hour on a stationary treadmill. "You can't tell the bosses from the workers because everyone's a worker and everyone's a boss." The uniform of the day is mostly T-shirts and blue jeans, with an impressive number of employees preferring well-worn Harley-Davidson T-shirts. Clearly this is a factory that works on the principle of mutual respect, from management to workforce and back.

The York final assembly plant turns out a new Harley-Davidson motorcycle from start to finish in two hours and twenty-four minutes. One motorcycle comes off the assembly line every two-and-a-half minutes. Each day the plant working on three shifts turns out 570 motorcycles made to customer order. The new Harley plant in Kansas City turns out 250 motorcycles a day, and still demand exceeds supply. The tour itself takes the better part of an hour, and by the end of it you are bound to be a new member of the Harley cult, even if you ride a rice burner. Tours are free and begin hourly. Afterward you return to the visitor center where you're invited to sit on a new Harley model and dream.

Harley-Davidson Corporate headquarters are in Milwaukee, Wisconsin, but Pennsylvania has been producing the majority of Harley-Davidson motorcycles since 1968. The York final assembly plant actually started life as a World War II munitions factory. In fact, there's still a fifty-year-old military-looking watchtower overlooking the visitor's parking lot. Harley-Davidson factory tours are Monday through Friday 10:00 A.M., 11:00 A.M., noon, 1:00 P.M., and 2:00 P.M.; 717–848–1177.

Mars •
Ford City • 422
Indiana •
Aliquippa
30
Loretto • Altoona • Culp •
Pittsburgh 22 Holidaysburg •
Latrobe • Drab •
Clairton Johnstown •
Canonsburg SOUTHWEST • Windber
Washington 70 New Paris •
Monessen 76
40
19 Connellsville New Baltimore • Bedford
Uniontown 30 220 70 522
119 Fairchance 219
522
76 To
11

SOUTHWEST

# SOUTHWEST

## THE CURVE THAT MADE A CITY
### Altoona

Altoona has been famous for 150 years for one thing, a bend in the railroad tracks called the Horseshoe Curve. In fact, the only reason there is a city called Altoona (Cherokee for "highlands of great worth") is that the Pennsylvania Railroad decided to cross the Allegheny Mountains in 1850. Up until that time, a trip from Philadelphia to Pittsburgh took three days, in an ingenious but almost comically complicated series of transfers from train to boat to train to boat. You'd start out by train in Philadelphia and travel to Columbia in Lancaster County, where you'd board a mule-pulled canal boat up the Susquehanna River. After negotiating a series of eighteen locks, you'd arrive in Holidaysburg in Blair County, where you would board the Allegheny Portage Railroad, which carried the entire canal boat over the mountains to Johnstown in Cambria County. There, an inclined railroad deposited the canal boats and passengers into the Conemaugh River for the final leg of the journey through sixty-six canal locks to Pittsburgh.

There had to be a better way. The problem was that the mountains were too steep for a train to climb and too wide to tunnel through. It took a Pennsylvania Railroad engineer by the name of J. Edgar Thompson to come up with the idea of building a curve into a V-shaped wedge carved out of the mountain in the middle of the nowhere that was to become Altoona.

*A curve so famous they named a beer after it (the Horseshoe Curve in Altoona).*

Construction started in 1851 and was accomplished by several hundred Irish immigrants using gunpowder, pickaxes, and pack animals. The massive earth-moving project was literally done by hand. The 220-degree curve is 2,374 feet long. There distance between the tracks on either side of the U shape of the curve is 1,800 feet. The tracks rise 91 feet per mile, and the west side of the curve is 122 feet higher than the east side. Without the curve, the grade over the mountains would have been six to eight degrees, which would have worn out engines and brakes. With the curve, the grade over the mountains is a manageable 1.8 percent. When it opened in 1854, the Horseshoe Curve was considered an engineering marvel. Virtually all train traffic, both passenger and freight, heading to Philadelphia from the west still uses the two remaining tracks through the curve.

The Horseshoe Curve National Historical Landmark is located five miles west of Altoona up a winding stretch of road past the Kittanning Reservoir. On the ride up the mountain, Molly and I saw a black bear standing in the middle of the road. It was the most exciting thing we saw. The irony of the curve built for trains and named after a horse's footwear is that it is best seen from an airplane. There is no grand vista available from the opposite slope of the mountain. You can't see the curve from street level, and when you do take the short incline ride from the Horseshoe Curve Visitor's Center to the track bed 90 feet above, you can't see the curve from there either. Standing there at the bottom of the U in the curve, all you can see are railroad tracks that bend in the distance in either direction until they are obscured by trees. If you're lucky, a train might pass, but the sight looks remarkably like a train passing. The only difference is the screech of the train wheel flanges holding on to the curve as the train rounds the bend and disappears into the trees. Maybe the dead of winter is the best time to visit the Horseshoe Curve. All that pesky Pennsylvania foliage spoils the view.

## WHY ALTOONA?
### Altoona

If one picture speaks a thousand words, then the expression on my daughter Molly's face speaks two: Not again! It must be hard for a ten-year-old to travel for hours across the state, rarely taking her eyes off her Game Boy to look at the mountains, and finally arrive at our destination only to discover that it's not an amusement park but a *museum*. A museum about *trains*, no less. (A little boy museum, if ever there was one.)

*Like most people in the 1920s, Babe Ruth traveled to Altoona by train.*

The Altoona Railroaders Memorial Museum is much more than a collection of antique locomotives. It is a stirring tribute to a way of life. Altoona started as a working village carved out of a wilderness by necessity and the accident of geography. It became a city, one of the largest in the state, and was one of Pennsylvania's proud industrial workshops until its inevitable decline after World War II. "Railroaders" is the key word in the name of this museum. It's about the people who worked for the Pennsylvania Railroad, it's about life in a railroad town when locomotives ruled the rails.

"A dirty city was a good city because it meant people were working," says Sally Price, a railroad employee featured in one of the exhibits. "We always considered it gold dust, not coal

dust. That's what made Altoona run." What made Altoona run
was what made Altoona filthy in its heyday, when hundreds of
smoke-belching locomotives passed through town on the sixty-
four eastbound tracks and seventy-two westbound tracks that
dominated the middle of town where the 218 acres of the Pennsylvania Railroad repair shops were located.

Today the museum stands where the great locomotives were
once serviced. On the second floor you'll see a life-size figure of
a woman crossing the Twelfth Street bridge as the trains pass
underneath, causing the kind of updraft made famous by Marilyn Monroe standing over a subway vent in *The Seven Year
Itch*. The figure must have been that of a city girl, because the
caption information noted that country girls held down their
skirts in the updraft, while city girls held on to their hats.
Another item of interest is a classy-looking metal device about
the size of an eyeglasses screwdriver. It has a wire loop at the
end that was used to remove burning cinders from a person's
eyes. (Railroaders Memorial Museum, 1300 Ninth Avenue,
Altoona; 817–946–0834. Open 9:00 A.M. to 5:00 P.M. Monday
through Sunday April–October; closed Monday
November–March. Admission charged.

### FINDING FORT ROBERDEAU
#### Culp

**M**y daughter Molly and I were driving from Altoona to
Lock Haven along I–99 when I spotted a sign that said
FORT ROBERDEAU HISTORIC LANDMARK 8 MILES. Pennsylvania had
almost as many forts as Carter had pills—Fort Pitt, Fort Necessity, Fort LeBoeuf, Fort Mifflin—most dating from Colonial
times. But I had never heard of Fort Roberdeau. Was it French?
What was it defending?

"Wanna go look for Fort Roberdeau?" I asked my ten-year-old. "Aurgh!" Molly groaned, not at my question but at the treacherous turn of events on the Game Boy she'd been hunched over for the last 40 miles. I took that as a yes.

Now, something odd happens when you turn off the main road in search of something you've never seen or heard of. What does a "Historic Landmark" look like? We exited I–99 at Bellwood and then wound our way up Brush Mountain on State Route 1008. Near the top of the mountain, the view of Sinking Spring Valley opens up below, and I figured Fort Roberdeau must have defended the heights or something. But

*One of the many signs showing the way to the elusive Fort Roberdeau.*

down the other side of the mountain we went, Molly emitting
an occasional "aurgh," through the village of Skelp, where we
turned right on State Route 1015 heading toward the village of
Culp. (What? No expressway between Skelp and Culp?!) I was
beginning to fear that the next village would be Gulp, when I
saw another FORT ROBERDEAU HISTORIC LANDMARK sign pointing
right on Kettle Road. About a half mile farther was another
much bigger sign pointing to the Fort Roberdeau. I turned
right, and there, about a hundred yards up the road, was one
of those blue and yellow Pennsylvania historical markers in the
middle of a cornfield. "Fort Roberdeau," it said. "Site of the
Revolutionary fort built by Gen. Daniel Roberdeau in 1778 to
protect to Sinking Valley lead mines . . . ."

Well, that was a long way to go for a short sign. At least
that's what I thought at the time. It turns out that there is an
actual wooden fort, a restoration of the original Fort
Roberdeau, built during the 1976 Bicentennial, a few hundred
yards farther up the road. But I didn't discover that until after
we got home. The original Fort Roberdeau was a fortified
stockade designed to protect the lead mining operation crucial
to the Continental Army's need for ammunition. Miners were
threatened by Indians and British sympathizers, but there is no
record of any attacks on Fort Roberdeau, which was known as
the Lead Mines Fort by the locals. Historically, Fort Roberdeau
was what you might call a "one-year wonder." Not only wasn't
there any real pressing need for such a garrison due to enemy
activity, but the lead mining operations of the limestone strata
of Sinking Springs Valley was more trouble than it was worth.
Once the French signed on as American allies in 1778, the
need for locally manufactured ammunition was lessened. By
the summer of 1779, Fort Roberdeau was abandoned by its garrison, which was needed for duty elsewhere.

Fort Roberbeau is open from mid-May to mid-October. I suggest first calling the fort at (814) 946–0048 to check its hours,
although you can see that sign in the cornfield anytime.

# THE MOTHER
# OF ALL HIGHWAYS

*"Most baby boomers, and even more of their children, have never heard of the Lincoln Highway," concludes a history of America's first transcontinental automobile roadway, published by the Lincoln Highway Association. Being a baby boomer, I took this personally. Whaddaya mean, "never heard of the Lincoln Highway"?! Everyone knows about the Lincoln Highway, right? Certainly every Pennsylvanian should have heard of it, considering that eighty-four communities, from Oxford Valley in Bucks County on the east to Smith's Ferry in Beaver County to the west, are part of the Pennsylvania route of the original Lincoln Highway that linked New York with San Francisco.*

*Then I realized that I'm a little biased, considering that I grew up less than a mile away from the Lincoln Highway, which is called Lancaster Avenue from the Philadelphia area westward to the Lanscaster area, where it becomes Philadelphia Pike. By whatever name it is known locally (in Greensburg, Westmoreland County, it's called Pittsburgh Street), the Route 30 portion of the Lincoln Highway meanders for 320 miles across the southern tier of Pennsylvania through some of the most spectacular scenery in the state.*

*The plan for a transcontinental automobile route was adopted in 1912. It was scheduled for completion in 1915, in time for the Panama-Pacific Exposition hosted in San Francisco. The chief advocate for what he called the Coast-to-Coast Highway was Carl Fisher, owner of the Indianapolis Motor Speedway, who proposed that the roadway be built with private funds. It wasn't until Henry Joy, president of the Packard Motor Car Co., came up with the idea of nam-*

*Mister Ed's Elephant Museum and candy store, midway between Gettysburg and*
*Chambersburg on the Lincoln Highway, is home to a vast array of elephant*
*trinkets and figurines collected by Mr. Ed over the years.*

*ing the highway for Abraham Lincoln that funds began*
*pouring in. Pennsylvania is pivotal in the cross-country*
*route that starts at Times Square in New York City and*
*heads south through New Jersey and into Pennsylvania*
*along Route 1. In Philadelphia, the Lincoln Highway makes*
*its big west turn toward the left coast on Route 30, and the*
*route number doesn't change until it becomes I–80 in*
*Granger, Wyoming.*

*"We're thirteen years older and 1,000 miles longer than*
*Route 66, but for some reason fewer people seem to know*
*about the Lincoln Highway," says Olga Herbert. "I guess we*
*needed a popular TV show named after it." Herbert is the*
*executive director of the Lincoln Highway Heritage Corridor,*

(continued)

a state-sponsored organization that is part of the Pennsylvania Heritage Parks Program. The corridor embraces 200 miles of the Lincoln Highway, through mostly rural and mountainous sections of Pennsylvania, from the York County line on the east to the Allegheny County line on the west. In between are some of roadside Pennsylvania's kitschiest sights, such as the two-story-tall diner shaped like a coffeepot in Bedford and the hotel shaped like a steamship at the summit of

*At Mister Ed's Elephant Museum and candy store, shoplifting is punished severely.*

Allegheny Mountain. In coming years the Lincoln Highway Heritage Corridor, which was created in 1995, will try to promote more public awareness of the highway's history and its attractions. Already the corridor is marked by 152 distinctive signs that resemble the 3,000 concrete markers that were placed virtually every mile along the original coast-to-coast Lincoln Highway. The new signs have a big blue L with a Lincoln penny above it.

# *N* UDIST *V* OLLEYBALL *S* UPER *B* OWL *XXX*
## *D a r l i n g t o n*

They've been playing nudist volleyball in Beaver County since the White Thorn Lodge opened in rural Darlington in 1962. Since 1971 the fame of White Thorn's annual week-after-Labor-Day-weekend buck-nekkid volleyball competition had spread throughout nudist circles so that it achieved the status of the official Nudist Volleyball Super Bowl. The thirtieth annual will be held in September 2001, but this naked Super Bowl XXX isn't X-rated. It's a family affair that attracts up to 1,500 nude volleyball enthusiasts each year.

Teams play in a round-robin tournament that lasts the better part of two days on the lodge's eleven volleyball courts. Not all the competitors are practicing nudists. "You can tell the ones who aren't," said White Thorn President Lawrence Hettinger. "We call them 'cottontails'," a reference to the tan lines so conspicuous among nonnudists.

Still, there are some seeming incongruities at a Nudist Volleyball Super Bowl. Souvenir T-shirts, for instance. And if you're looking to identify your favorite team by their uniforms, forget it. It's all skins all the time. One nice touch is the nude barbecue grills over at Walt's Wonderful World of Burgers, where Walt Lippert serves up hamburgers while wearing nothing but an apron to protect himself from grease splatter. "We may be nudists," said Walt, "but we're not stupid."

The Nudist Volleyball Super Bowl attracts competitors from as far away as Florida, California, and Canada, and the competition is broken down by skill levels. There are men's, women's, and coed divisions. Up to ninety teams participate. Admission is $25 per person and, although clothing is optional, it is frowned upon.

## *EVERYONE KNOWS IT'S SLINKY*
### *Hollidaysburg*

Who knew? Certainly not Richard James who invented it.
And not his wife, Betty, who named it. And not even the first
customers who bought out the entire inventory during a
Christmas shopper demonstration at Gimbel's Department Store
in Philadelphia in 1945. Who knew that a simple spring in a
box would become one of the most recognizable toys in the
world, an American icon made in Pennsylvania called the
Slinky? Who knew that the Slinky would become part of the
Smithsonian Institution's permanent Americana exhibit? Who
knew that the United States Postal Service would honor the
Slinky with its own postage stamp in 1999? Who knew it
would take a world war to inspire an invention that has lasted
longer than the Third Reich?

> "It's Slinky! It's Slinky! For fun it's a wonderful toy.
> It's Slinky! It's Slinky! It's fun for a girl and a boy.
> Everyone knows it's Slinky!"

Everyone knows the Slinky jingle. At least 90 percent of the
American adults polled in 1995 knew the jingle, probably
because they owned a Slinky as a child or because they had
bought one for their own children. Today the sales of Slinky
Toys by James Industries in Hollidaysburg in Blair County
have equaled the population of the United States—closing in on
300 million. That's a lot of shhhhiIINGG shhhiiIINGGing down
the stairs.

It all started during World War II at the Philadelphia Naval
Shipyard. In 1943 a young Penn State graduate named
Richard James was working as a naval engineer, trying to
develop a system to stabilize sensitive monitoring equipment

aboard ships in pitching seas. James was experimenting with springs of various sizes when, as the story goes, he noticed one spring fall off a stack of books, uncoiling itself and then righting itself on the book below, before continuing its journey to the next level. "Radar-shmadar," James may or may not have muttered to himself, but in any language it was "Eureka."

For the next couple of years, when he wasn't working to bring the Axis powers to their knees, James worked on his postwar plans to bring millions of kids to their knees to play with his toy without a name. Betty James scoured the dictionary looking for a word that fit the toy. She chose "slinky" because it meant "stealthy, sleek, and sinuous"—not to mention sibilant.

Slinky it was. A name as simple and delightful as the toy. In 1945 Richard James borrowed $500 to pay a local machine shop to press wire into a coil, 80 feet of wire per coil. He badgered Gimbel's buyers into allowing him to demonstrate his toy to Christmas shoppers, using a portable set of stairs. In ninety minutes, his entire stock of 400 Slinkies was sold at one dollar a Slinky. And so it began.

The Slinky story isn't entirely a happy one, although it has remained a family one. In 1960 Richard James abandoned his wife and six children to pursue what his children describe as a "missionary cult" in Bolivia. He nearly bankrupted James Industries in the process with his contributions to the cult. Betty James packed up her children and moved back to her family and hometown roots Hollidaysburg, where Slinkies have been manufactured ever since, using the same equipment designed by Richard James. Betty, now in her eighties, is still the CEO of James Industries, which is managed by son Thomas James.

I had to ask about something that has bothered me ever since I followed my first Slinky down the stairs. "What do you call it when the coils of a Slinky get tangled together?" I asked. "Is there a technical name for that?"

"Yes," replied Thomas James. "It's called broken."

## *FLOODTOWN, USA*
### *Johnstown*

T he last survivor of the original Johnstown Flood died in
1997 at the age of 108. His name was Frank Shomo and he
died in his sleep, just as certainly as he would have died as a
sleeping infant more than a century earlier when the wall of
water arrived at his house 20 miles downstream and a county
away from Johnstown, Pennsylvania. His father saved him, and
Frank Shomo never tired of telling the story he was too young to
remember, but which would become the defining story of his life.

Talk about defining stories. Who among us can hear the
name Johnstown without immediately adding the word *flood*?
What Chicago is to "Fire" and what San Francisco is to "Earthquake," Johnstown is to floods. Not once. Not twice. But three
times. All during Frank Shomo's lifetime.

The original Johnstown Flood in 1889 killed twice as many
people as the Chicago Fire of 1871 and the San Francisco
Earthquake of 1906 *combined!* The official number of dead is
listed at 2,209, placing it second in mortality among disasters
in United States history, behind the horrific hurricane in Galve-
ston, Texas, in 1900 that claimed upwards of 6,000 lives.

The cruel irony of the Johnstown tragedy was that nearly
as many people died from fire as from water. After 24 hours of
torrential rainfall, the dam broke on the earthen reservoir on
the South Branch of the Conemaugh River. It happened a little
after three o'clock in the afternoon on May 31, 1889. The dike
collapsed and a wall of water 75 feet high and a half mile wide
swept through town, breaking gas mains as it carried away
buildings, igniting floating debris trapped beneath bridges,
creating an inferno atop the deluge.

It was the biggest story in America since the Civil War. A newspaper reporter from New York wired back a story from Johnstown that began, "God stood on a mountain top . . ." to which his editor wired back, "Forget flood. Interview God." In Philadelphia, soon-to-be internationally famous reporter Richard Harding Davis wrote dispatches from Johnstown describing the discovery of a prisoner found drowned in his locked cell in the local pokey. A catcher's mask lying in the mud, wrote Harding Davis, looked like it had been "hastily flung off to catch a foul ball."

The Johnstown Flood National Memorial is located at the base of what remains of the dam that burst that deadly day in 1889. The infant Frank Shomo was a man in his late forties when the second great flood struck Johnstown on St. Patrick's Day in 1936, killing twenty-five. It had been a cold winter, piling up 14 feet of snow that didn't begin to melt until a storm accompanied by 50-degree weather struck in mid-March. The river swelled to 17 feet above normal.

Then there was the bizarre event of July 20, 1977, when what was supposed to be a passing storm system hovered over Johnstown like a bad check. In nine hours the stalled storm dropped almost a foot of rain. Three dams broke. Eighty-five people died. Frank Shomo, then a mere eighty-seven, had to be physically evacuated, protesting all the while that he'd seen worse than this before.

Even as government disaster crews were rushing to Johnstown after the deadly 1977 flood, local entrepreneurs had put a smile on the face of catastrophe. Street-corner hucksters were selling souvenir T-shirts bearing the message "Floods–3, Johnstown–0."

## ROLLING ROCK
### AND THE MYSTERY OF "33"
#### Latrobe

Latrobe is a mighty metropolis (NOT!) of fewer than 10,000 residents in Westmoreland County, roughly halfway between Pittsburgh and Johnstown. What Pittsburgh was to steel and Johnstown was to floods, Latrobe continues to be to beer. Or at least, to beer "mystique."

Perhaps the most unbelievable scene in the movie *The Deerhunter* wasn't the riveting Russian roulette scene with Robert DeNiro and Christopher Walken, it was the wedding scene at the VFW Post bar in Clairton, Pennsylvania, when Robert DeNiro has to explain to Meryl Streep what Rolling Rock beer is. Duh-UH! Who in Pennsylvania, especially in western Pennsylvania, doesn't know about "the glass-lined tanks of Old Latrobe," about the solemn pledge, "We tender this premium beer for your enjoyment" because it is "a tribute to your good taste"? Who, I ask you?

Nobody. Which is the same answer to the question, "Who knows what the '33' means on the back of the Rolling Rock bottle?" Theories? Yes, there are theories galore and if you call Latrobe Brewing Company you'll get an automated voice that lists a menu of options, including, "For theories about the mysterious '33' that appears on the back of the Rolling Rock bottle, press 8." There you will hear the usual litany:

1. The "33" signifies the year Prohibition ended, 1933.
2. There are 33 letters in the words that make up the beer's ingredients: malt, rice, corn, brewer's yeast, water.
3. There are 33 words on the back label of the Rolling Rock bottle.

The automated message ends with the enigmatic conclusion, "And so you see, it's still a mystery."

The story of why Rolling Rock seven-ounce bottles are called "ponies" is easy enough. There's an illustration of a horse on all Rolling Rock bottles (a reference to the steeplechase races that were popular on the Mellon family property near Latrobe). The original brown twelve-ounce bottle was called a "horse" and the smaller green bottles naturally became known as ponies. Rolling Rock switched from brown to green glass during World War II to make it easier for bartenders to recognize which bottles to return to Latrobe. "For some reason," the company noted, "not many Becks were being consumed in the states at the time."

Latrobe Brewing Co. does not offer tours of the actual brewing facility, but there is a gift shop and visitors' center where you can watch a twelve-minute movie about Rolling Rock Beer and then tour a small museum of collectibles. The visitor's center at 119 Jefferson Street, Latrobe, is open Monday through Friday 9:00 A.M. to 5:00 P.M., Saturday 9:00 A.M. to 3:00 P.M.; call (724) 537–5545.

## MR. SMITH GOES TO LORETTO
### Loretto

Before America's first saint, Bishop John Neumann, ever set foot in Philadelphia, another immigrant priest had already spent forty years in Western Pennsylvania, where his memory among frontier Catholics has been raised to near-saint status. One day, perhaps, Fr. Demetrius Gallitzin, known as the Apostle of the Alleghenies, will join St. John Neumann and St. Katherine Drexel as Pennsylvania's officially canonized members. As it is now, his memory lives on as a 4,000-acre state park in Cambria County, Prince Gallitzin State Park.

Prince Gallitzin, a member of Russian royalty and son of the Czar's attaché to France and Holland, came to America in the wake of the French Revolution. He was a recent and devout convert to Catholicism and he studied for the priesthood in the Diocese of Baltimore, where he became the second man ordained to the priesthood in the United States. Preferring to downplay his royal Russian background, Prince Gallitzin used an Americanized nom de clergy, "Mr. Rev. Smith." In 1799 Archbishop Carroll of Baltimore asked Mr. Rev. Smith to travel to Western Pennsylvania and establish a parish among a small group of Catholics living in the mountain wilderness. The undercover prince built a log church in Loretto, Cambria County, and ministered to a congregation scattered over hundreds of square miles. During Gallitzin's lifetime, Bishop Kendrick of Philadelphia described him as "a priest whose pure and humble life excites [Catholics] to the exercise of the evangelical virtues."

By the time he died at the age of seventy, on Easter Sunday, 1840—twelve years before St. John Neumann was consecrated Bishop of Philadelphia—five priests were assisting the princely priest Gallitzin in his missionary work. Loretto, a town of just over 1,000 people, is still considered one of the founding shrines of Catholicism in Western Pennsylvania. According to a magazine article about Prince Gallitzin published by the St. Benedict Center, "The little town of Loretto, Pennsylvania, which he founded, continues to be one of the most Catholic towns in America, as evinced by its ten Catholic Churches and three monasteries."

## A TOWN CALLED MARS
### Mars

Life in Mars is pretty much the same as life in any other small town in western Pennsylvania. The only difference is that visitors passing through other towns aren't apt to greet locals with "Nanoo, nonoo" or "Take me to your leader." Last fall, the Fightin' Planets of the Mars Area High School football team finished up a disappointing six-and-four season, but native Martians took it in stride. According to Lester Kennedy, who wrote about life in Mars for the town's centennial booklet published in 1973, "Mars is situated 55 miles southwest of Venus (Pa.); 1,875 miles northeast of Mercury (Nev.), and 925 miles north of Jupiter (Fla.). It is approximately 35 million miles, at point of closest approach, from the planet Mars."

More prosaically, Mars is 18 miles north of Pittsburgh and 12 miles southwest of Butler. Except for its uncommon name, Mars is typical of thousands of small towns strewn across the length and breadth of America.

Mars (population 1,713) is a borough not quite a half mile square in the southern part of Butler County. Its claims to fame are its name and an aluminum flying saucer modeled after Warner Brothers cartoon character Marvin the Martian's, which usually sits in the town square on Grand Avenue, although it's small enough for teenage pranksters to move it around town from time to time. There's a blue Pennsylvania town marker in downtown Mars that is inaccurate on two counts. It says, MARS, NAMED AFTER THE STAR OF MARS. FOUNDED 1876. Upon last sighting, Mars was a planet, not a star, the fourth rock from the sun. And Mars dates its incorporation as a community to the opening of the Mars post office in 1873 in the home of one Samuel Parks. The origin of the name Mars is also disputed. The minority opinion is that Mrs. Parks was a student of astronomy and suggested the name. The majority opinion is that Mars was chosen to honor the political patron responsible for Mr. Parks winning the post office contract, the Hon. Samuel Marshall. For a brief period in 1877, the town was on the verge of being named Overbrook, because of the opening of a B&O Railroad station bearing that name, but because there was already an Overbrook post office in Philadelphia (also named after a Pennsylvania Railroad train station), the name Mars stuck.

Today, Martians tend to live more comfortably with their alien identities than the citizens of, say, Roswell, New Mexico.

# *WHAT, NO GALAXY, PENNSYLVANIA?*

*There's an Atlas in Northumberland County, which is as good a place as any to start a tour of the world and the near solar system, courtesy of Pennsylvania towns with names like Moon, Mars, and Venus. A traveler crossing the state might scratch his head and check the road map, "I didn't know Dallas was in Pennsylvania. And Houston. And Austin. Not to mention Denver, Brooklyn, Milwaukee, Sacramento, Richmond, and Buffalo!"*

*There's a Frisco, Pennsylvania, but no San Francisco. There's a Bangor and a Salem and a Reno and a Knoxville, but they aren't followed by Maine, Massachusetts, Nevada, or Tennessee. Entire states have a Pennsylvania after their names. There's a California, a Virginia, an Idaho, an Iowa, an Indiana, and even an Oklahoma, which is appropriate because*

*the most famous Oklahoman is buried in the*
*Pennsylvania town that bears his name, Jim Thorpe.*
*There's both a Yukon and an Alaska, Pennsylvania.*
*Americans of Irish descent can visit Dublin,*
*Belfast, Ulster, Munster, Donegal, Sligo, Waterford,*
*and Derry without ever leaving Pennsylvania. There's*
*even an Irishtown and a Paddytown. German*
*Americans will feel right at home in Germany, Berlin,*
*East Berlin, Hamburg, Nuremburg, and not one but*
*two Germantowns, a Germanville, and a Germania.*
*Homesick Scots can go to either Glasgow or Scotland,*
*with maybe a side trip to Brogue. Italians can tour*
*Milan, Rome, Verona, and Florence, not to mention*
*Little Italy neighborhoods in cities across the state.*
*There's a Frenchville and a Paris too, and if Gallic*
*pride can handle a visit, Pennsylvania also has its*
*own Waterloo.*

*There's an English Center, Pennsylvania, as well as*
*London, Oxford, Cambridge, Lancaster, York, and*
*Nottingham. Pennsylvania has its Gibraltar and its*
*Corsica and Malta too. There's a Poland and a*
*Warsaw. There's a Moscow and a St. Petersburg.*
*There's a Dalmatia and a Bohemia and a Macedonia*
*and a Moravia. There's Athens and Sparta and even*
*Troy. South of the border but still in the state are*
*Mexico, Lima, and Santiago. To the north (but not*
*that far north) are Finland, Sweden, Ottawa, Halifax,*
*and Newfoundland, Pennsylvania.*

*The Middle East is well represented in this Middle*
*Atlantic state. There's Egypt and Luxor and Jericho*
*and Palestine and Hebron and Galilee and Bethlehem*
*and Nazareth and Jewtown. There's Bagdad and*
*Tripoli and Crete. Unlike their Middle Eastern*
*namesakes, these communities aren't likely to go to*
*war with each other. But if they did, they could*
*always work out a peace agreement at Geneva,*
*Pennsylvania.*

STEP ON UP TO THE
*"CHURCH ON THE TURNPIKE"*
New Baltimore

The Pennsylvania Turnpike has 512 miles, five tunnels, 55 interchanges, 22 service plazas, and one Catholic church. In fact, the Pennsylvania Turnpike may be the only limited-access toll road in the country that has steps leading from the shoulder of the highway up an embankment and into a church. You can see the steps on either side of the turnpike at Mile Marker 129 in New Baltimore between the Bedford and Somerset exits.

So what's up with that? The "Church on the Turnpike," as St. John the Baptist Catholic Church has become known to countless travelers over the years, was founded by German immigrants in 1824. The church building itself, which stands about 100 yards off the south side of the turnpike, was built in 1890. It resembles a miniature European cathedral and was built by hand by artisans from the parish. In 1937 when the right-of-way for the Pennsylvania Turnpike was being sur-veyed, the route chosen for the new highway cut right through the cemetery of St. John's eighty-acre plot in Somerset County. A deal was struck between the Turnpike Commission and the Trustees of St. John's. The existing graves would be excavated and moved in exchange for access in perpetuity for travelers on the turnpike who wanted to stop at the church. Concrete steps with metal railings were built up the side of the embankments on both east- and westbound lanes (the latter steps lead up to the Findley Street overpass).

The deal was struck in good faith and has never been rescinded. The church is frequently visited by travelers pulling over to the shoulder when they see the large lighted cross of St. John's beckoning from the side of the turnpike. The church's message sign with its schedule of masses is turned toward the highway, and according to St. John's pastor, Fr. Mark Begly, most "off turnpike" Mass-goers prefer to attend the 6:00 Saturday evening mass or the 10:30 Sunday morning mass. "I get a lot of people who come off the turnpike during the day looking for someone to hear their confession," said Fr. Begly. "They've been traveling and maybe they've done some things they wish they hadn't done and they want to confess in a place where they're not known and they'll never be seen again."

Truckers like the lighted cross outside St. John's because it is a landmark midway between the Bedford and Somerset exits. A couple of years ago, the lights on the cross were broken, and Fr. Begly said that he received phone calls from passing truckers offering to help pay for new lights for their nighttime beacon. The parish paid for the new lights without the truckers' contributions.

The most unlikely "off turnpike" support for the church came from Charles "Chick" Curry, a retired IBM computer service specialist, who had been driving past St. John's during his trips across the state since the 1950s. What caught Curry's eye was not the steps so much as the clock tower on the church. The hands on the six-foot clock face never moved. Curry was a clock buff since childhood and had become an accomplished clock maker. One day in 1999 on his way home to Delaware, he finally decided to find out once and for all why the clock didn't work. He pulled over on the turnpike shoulder and climbed the steps to the church, which, to his surprise, was well tended and in good repair. He explained his interest to Fr. Begley, who showed him the reason the hands never moved. The clock's hands were bolted to the face. There was no time-keeping mechanism inside the clock tower. There never had been.

Curry (a "raised Presbyterian") offered to build a clockworks for the church. He even offered to build a mechanism to ring the church bell on the hour. And he offered to do it for free. "They didn't think I was for real," Curry said of the reaction from St. John's parishioners to his offer. But he was for real. It took him three to four months to design and build a clockworks and bell-ringing mechanism. "It's a ten-pound sledgehammer, actually," he said of the bell clapper. He even cut, shaped, sanded, and varnished new minute and hour hands from redwood to match the nonfunctional steel hands.

After a two-month test of the electrically powered clock in the church's community room, Curry's clockworks were installed in the tower and officially dedicated on October 29, 2000. "It begins striking the hour at exactly eight seconds before the hour," Curry said. "Sometimes I'll call up there and look at my master clock and I'll say, 'You should hear it start chiming in three . . . two . . . one . . . now!' And I'll hear it over the phone."

## *In Search of Gravity Hill*
### *New Paris*

I was on the verge of summoning Leonard Nimoy to help me solve the mystery of Gravity Hill. The mystery wasn't what happens at Gravity Hill (water flows uphill, cars on a downhill slope roll backward) or even why that happens (scientifically speaking, there is no explanation, although optical illusion is the most cited reason), but rather *where* Gravity Hill is in Pennsylvania.

Gravity Hill was one of the first "curiosities" I was urged to find by callers to a Philadelphia radio talk show I was hosting. "It's somewhere in Bucks County," I was told, "up near Yardley." Other callers disagreed. "No, it's near New Hope," said another. "No, it's definitely in Warrington." People knew exactly where it was but they couldn't tell me how to get there. I started calling police stations in the area, figuring that if there was a Gravity Hill in the neighborhood, the cops would know about it. Some did, some didn't. But it was always in the next town over.

I began asking people I'd meet in my travels around the state. "Yeah, there's one of them in Lancaster County," said Larry Homan, a chainsaw sculptor. "Water flows uphill. It's a road in the middle of a cornfield." I never gave up on finding Gravity Hill, wherever it was, but I was beginning to think it was a rural myth. Then, as luck would have it, I came across a brochure for the Bedford County Visitors' Bureau touting "Gravity Hill, New Paris, Pa." When I told Dennis Tice, director of the Bedford County Visitors Bureau, how long I'd been looking for Gravity Hill in Bucks County, he deadpanned, "Yeah, we bought it from them and moved it up here." Directions to Gravity Hill are available on the Bedford County Visitors Bureau Web site (www.bedfordcounty.net/Gravityhill/index.htm) but be forewarned, it's not easy to find. You've got to take a couple of unmarked forks in tiny back roads then travel two tenths of a mile until you see a big GH spray painted on the road. Go another tenth of a mile until you see another GH, and you have arrived. Put the car in neutral and it will roll uphill. Pour water on the ground, it will flow uphill rather than down. About a quarter mile farther up the road is *another* Gravity Hill (talk about an embarrassment of riches—or is it anomalies?). Why the spray painted GH on the road? Evidently the law of gravity wasn't the only law being broken. "We used to put up signs but they ended up getting stolen," said Tice. "This is cheaper."

Gravity Hill is by no means unique to Pennsylvania. In fact, the phenomenon has become fairly well commercialized in other states. They go by different names: Spook Hill in Lake Wells, Florida; Mystery Spot in Santa Cruz, California; the Oregon Vortex in Gold Hill, Oregon; and Gravity Hill in Mooreville, Indiana, to name a few.

## THE THREE RIVERS FERRY
### Pittsburgh

Thousands of people in Pittsburgh take a boat to get to Steelers football games. It's the best way to beat the traffic on game day. For five dollars you can get a round-trip ticket on the ferry-size water taxis that shuttle back and forth across the Monongahela River from South Side to the stadium complex on the north side of the Allegheny River opposite downtown Pittsburgh.

I took the football ferry packed with Steelers fans to one of the last home games to be played at Three Rivers Stadium in 2000. It was a rainy Sunday in October and the opposition, the then winless Cincinnati Bengals, was as dreary as the weather. But the fans were upbeat, even the Bengals fans, one of who carried a sign that said, I'LL GO ANYWHERE FOR THE BENGALS' FIRST WIN. Three Rivers Stadium was flanked by the construction sites of the two new stadiums being built to accommodate the Steelers and the Pirates. On the ferry ride across the river, I asked a fan what the new Steelers stadium would be called. "They're going to call it PNC Park," he said. "That's because they have windows in the men's rooms and ladies' rooms." It took me a minute, but I got it.

Three Rivers was a saucer-shaped concrete bowl of the same age, style, and fate of Veterans Stadium in Philadelphia. Each city is replacing its single multipurpose stadiums with separate baseball and football stadiums a short distance from each other. Pittsburgh's Three Rivers area has always been associated with the city's professional sports. Two Pennsylvania historical markers were placed outside Three Rivers Stadium to commemorate America's first professional football game and the first World Series.

The first professional football game was played on November 12, 1892, in nearby Recreation Park between the Allegheny Athletic Association and the Pittsburgh Athletic Association. Allegheny won, with the winning touchdown being scored by William "Pudge" Heffelfinger, who was paid $500 to play. He was the first football player ever to be paid outright, and professional football dates its origin to that game. The first World Series was played at Exposition Park, on the site of Three Rivers Stadium, in October 1903 between the National League Pittsburgh Pirates and the American League champion Boston Pilgrims (later to be called the Red Sox). Games four through seven of the best-of-nine-game series were played on the site, featuring Hall of Famers Honus Wagner for Pittsburgh and Cy Young for Boston. The Pilgrims won the first World Series five games to three.

## AN UNLIKELY PITTSBURGH NATIVE
### Pittsburgh

Pop artist Andy Warhol's celebrated fifteen minutes of fame take up an entire seven floors of an industrial building in downtown Pittsburgh just a few blocks away from the house where he grew up. It's hard to say which is more unlikely, that a character like Warhol is a product of Pittsburgh, or that a city like Pittsburgh would be home to the Andy Warhol Museum if he weren't a hometown boy. The facts are that Warhol lived in Pittsburgh until leaving for New York to continue the art career he had begun while studying painting and design at the Carnegie Institute of Technology.

Andy Warhol was an odd chap, to say the least, and his oddness and his talent are on display at a museum devoted to his work on Sandusky Street not far from Pittsburgh's new stadi-

## DOMINIC AND EUGENE MEET BIRDY

*Two of my favorite movies of all time are set and shot in Philadelphia and Pittsburgh. The Philadelphia movie is* Birdy. *The Pittsburgh movie is* Dominic and Eugene. *They are enough to do a state proud.*

*I live in West Philadelphia, not far from where they filmed the opening sandlot baseball scenes in* Birdy, *which is a movie about unlikely friends who become brothers. I recognize by intuition the hilly Pittsburgh neighborhood streets traveled by the trash truck in* Dominic and Eugene, *which is about unlikely brothers who become friends and more.*

Birdy *stars Matthew Modine as the title character who raises pigeons and wants to fly like a bird, and Nicholas Cage as his friend Al, who raises girls' heartbeats and wants to know what Birdy knows about life and aerodynamics that he doesn't. It's hilarious and sad and wonderful and more Philadelphia than most movies ever touch. They've even got the William Penn statue joke in there. "Hey Birdy, remember when we'd get those old ladies to look up at City Hall tower?" asks Al as the camera shows The Founding Father in all his unintentional randiness (see page 66). Birdy and Al*

ums. He was a mamma's boy, Warhol was, and his mother joined him in New York following his father's death three years after he left Pittsburgh in 1949. Julia Warhola and her husband, Andrej, had immigrated to Pittsburgh from the Carpathian Mountain area of what is now Slovakia. Among the personal items on display in the Andy Warhol Museum are postcards the son sent his mother from his travels around the world. "Hi, Im alright im in Rome now its real nice here. Bye," he wrote in 1956. Other postcards with virtually the same unemotional and ungrammatical message were sent to his *go off to war (in the movie it's Vietnam, in the book it's World War II, in reality it doesn't matter) where Al loses half his face and Birdy loses half his mind, the remaining half being that of a bird. His better half.*

Dominic and Eugene *stars Tom Hulce and Ray Liotta as the title characters, the former being a beloved but obviously brain-injured municipal trash truck loader, the latter being his brilliant and loving but obviously stressed-out medical student twin brother. Jamie Lee Curtis is thrown in as a love interest, but it's really a story about brothers coming to grips with losing each other's company after all these years. One shiver-me-timbers moment of dialogue comes after Dominic's dog has been killed by a car. The trusting and innocent and inconsolable Dominic is praying before the altar of his parish church. After he rises from his knees to leave, a well-meaning parish priest tries to console him with hollow words about a doggie heaven. The now furious Pittsburgh trash man turns tail and stalks halfway up the aisle. Then he turns, glaring first at the priest and then at the crucified figure of Christ above the altar. "If I was God," he says, "I wouldn't let that happen to my boy."*

*I don't want to give away the ending to either movie (they're on video, people!) but I will tell you the final word of dialogue in* Birdy: *"What?"*

mother from other countries. Makes you wonder how the guy became so famous.

The answer to that is found in the 500 works of art that are on display, making the Andy Warhol Museum the most comprehensive lone-artist museum in the country. The pop art Campbell's soup can paintings are there, as well as the stylized portraits of Marilyn Monroe, Elvis, and Natalie Wood. The story of Warhol's life in the New York art and music and movie-making and magazine-publishing scene is told in various exhibits on different floors. His talent is undeniable.

*The "unlikely" Andy Warhol Museum in Pittsburgh.*

The Andy Warhol Museum, at 117 Sandusky Street, is open Tuesday through Sunday. Call (412) 237–8300.

### THE BLACK BABE RUTH
#### Pittsburgh

f Josh Gibson had been the same race as Babe Ruth, Forbes Field in Pittsburgh might have been called "The House That Gibson Built." But Josh Gibson was a black man playing baseball in the 1930s, the same era as the Babe, which meant that he couldn't play on the same team with white major-leaguers.

Instead, he played his entire baseball career for two of the greatest teams in Negro League history, the Pittsburgh Crawfords and the Homestead Grays.

Homestead is a steel town just a few miles downriver from Pittsburgh; the Negro League Grays played their home games at Forbes Field in Pittsburgh when the Pirates were out of town. The Grays signed a strapping eighteen-year-old from the North Side named Josh Gibson in July 1930. In that year's Negro League World Series between the Grays and the New York Lincoln Yankees, Gibson hit a home run over the 457-foot wall in left center field at Forbes Field, a feat that would not be repeated until thirty years later, when Mickey Mantle did it during the 1960 World Series. The following week the Negro League World Series shifted to New York, and Gibson became the only player ever to hit a ball out of Yankee stadium—a shot measured at an impossible 600 feet.

Catcher Josh Gibson was nicknamed the Black Bomber during a sixteen-year career in which he hit 800 home runs while batting over .300. When Gibson jumped over to the rival Pittsburgh Crawfords in 1932, he joined a team with five future Hall of Famers all playing at the same time, something not even the 1927 Yankees can claim. Besides Gibson, future Hall of Famers playing for the Crawfords included his battery mate Satchel Paige, Oscar Charleston, Judy Johnson, and "Cool Papa" Bell.

Gibson returned to the Grays in 1936 and finished his career in 1946, winning the Negro League batting title for the ninth time in his final year. The following year, Josh Gibson had a stroke caused by a brain tumor and died in his Strauss Street home on Pittsburgh's North Side. When Boston Red Sox slugger Ted Williams was inducted into the Baseball Hall of Fame in 1966, he said, "I hope that some day Satchel Paige and Josh Gibson will be voted into the Hall of Fame as symbols of the great Negro players who are not here only because they weren't given a chance." That day came in 1972. Josh Gibson was inducted into Major League Baseball's Hall of Fame despite never having played for a National or American League team.

Today in Pittsburgh, Josh Gibson's career is marked with a Pennsylvania historical marker at 2217 Bedford Avenue, where his baseball career started at Ammons Field.

### GREAT VIEW, IF YOU'RE SO INCLINED
*Pittsburgh*

Compact downtown Pittsburgh offers a dramatic skyline when seen from any angle, but perhaps the best and most dramatic view is from the top of Mt. Washington, the Pittsburgh neighborhood that looks down on the skyscrapers rising on the north side of the Monongahela River from its perch on a ridge on the south side. Looking up at the steep slope of Mt. Washington from the opposite shore, the expression "You can't get there from here" leaps to mind. A mountain goat might be able to. But you can too, if you're so inclined. And Pittsburghers have been so inclined for 130 years and counting.

The Duquesne Incline consists of two bus-size wooden structures that resemble Victorian-style private train cars from the late 1800s. The difference is that these cars travel vertically rather than horizontally. You might say that the Pittsburgh inclines were America's first urban elevated railways, but actually they were more like America's first mass transit elevators. The 400-foot ride on a 30-degree angle to the top of Mt. Washington takes two and a half minutes; the two cars heading in opposite directions pass each other midslope. Large windows—front, back, and side—offer spectacular views not to be missed by anyone untroubled by vertigo. A round-trip ride costs a dollar.

From the top of Mt. Washington, the city of Pittsburgh lays itself open like a huge oyster with a breathtaking pearl gleaming in the middle. To the west of the Allegheny River are the new Pirates and Steelers stadiums. In the middle is a glowing fountain, the centerpiece of Point State Park, where the Monon-

*At the Duquesne Incline in Pittsburgh, be careful what you say to the operator.*

gahela River meets the Allegheny to form the mighty Ohio River. To the west is downtown Pittsburgh, with its impressive skyscrapers, home to more national corporate headquarters than its cross-state big brother and rival Philadelphia. You can take it all in from the observation deck at the top of the Duquesne Incline. There's also a museum in the waiting room, telling the story of Pittsburgh's triumphs and travails.

At one time there were fifteen inclines serving the city and its working-class neighborhoods in the hills surrounding the riverside mills and factories. But after private automobiles became commonplace in the wake of World War II, one by one the inclines shut down. Only two inclines serve the city today. The Monongahela Incline, Pittsburgh's first, was built in 1870 and is still in operation about a mile west of the Duquesne Incline, which was built in 1877. In 1962 the Duquesne Incline, then operated by the city-owned transit company, was shut down because it was unprofitable. A year later the community rallied and took over the operation of the cable car system under the Society for the Preservation of the Duquesne Heights Incline. Today it is operated by friendly and enthsusiastic volunteers who recognize first-time travelers and ask how they liked their ride after the return trip. Seventy-five percent of the Duquesne Incline's riders these days are tourists rather than commuters.

There is one bit of Pittsburgh tradition that lives on among those with certain romantic inclinations. The Duquesne Incline is still a popular place for young Pittsburgh gentlemen to ask the ladies they love for their hand in marriage. Who could turn down a young man with the world at his feet? The hard part— getting an empty car in which to pop the question—is a lot easier if you have the right password to let the incline operator know a proposal is in the offing. "If you ask the right question, you can get a car that's empty except for the two of you," said David Miller, president of the Duquesne Incline preservation society. "The right question is, 'Fred Smith still work here?'" And don't ask unless you mean it.

# HAIL TO THE CHIEFS, PENNSYLVANIA

*There's a President, Pennsylvania, not too far from Polk, in Venango County. On your way from President to Polk on Route 62 you have to go through the town of Franklin. You can bypass Franklin on your way from President to Clinton in Fayette County, but you'll come perilously close to*

the nearby town of *Breakneck,* which somehow
seems appropriate. You can't get from President
to *Bush* or *Gore* because those towns don't exist,
which also seems appropriate.

The President–Clinton trip is one of the
President-to-president road trips in Pennsylvania.
You can travel from President to Truman in
Cameron County and President to Harding in
Luzerne County. Of course, you could also resign
yourself to drive from President to Nixon in
Susquehanna County.

Early American presidents are much better
represented. There's the President–Washington
trip, followed by President–Adams,
President–Jefferson, and President–Madison.
Those are the first four presidents in order, and
I suppose you could make it five if you added a
few hundred miles on the President–Adams trip
to include Quincy, located—interestingly—in
Franklin County. (The man was everywhere!) The
President–Monroe trip would be next, followed by
President–Jackson way up in Susquehanna
County. There is no Van Buren and no Harrison.
But the Presidential journeys pick up with
President–Tyler, President–Polk, and
President–Taylor.

Due to Pennsylvanians' good taste, there is no
President–Fillmore trip. Nor is there President–
Pierce. Nor, amazingly, President–Buchanan.
(James Buchanan was the only Pennsylvanian to
be elected president, which makes Pennsylvania
sort of the Phillies of presidential politics: one
winner in all those years.) President–Lincoln can
be driven in an afternoon, so can President–
Grant even if you add the side trip to Ulysses in
Potter County.

Towanda

NORTHEAST

Scranton • Archbald

L. Wallenpaupack

Kingston

Shickshinny •
Mocanaqua

Wilkes-Barre

Hazleton

Jim Thorpe • Pen Argyl

Mt. Carmel • Centralia
Pottsville

Easton

Allentown

Lehigh River

NORTHEAST

# NORTHEAST

## *THE WORLD'S LARGEST POTHOLE*
### *Archbald*

**P**ennsylvania has an official state bird (the ruffed grouse), an official state dog (great dane), an official state flower (mountain laurel), and an official state insect (the firefly). But did you know that Pennsylvania has commemorated something else so thoroughly indigenous to the Keystone State that cars bearing Firestone tires are turned away at the state line?

I speak of Pennsylvania's official state pothole. Contrary to the personal experience of locals, the official state pothole cannot be found in the passing lane of

*You thought you knew potholes? Here's Pennsylvania's Official State Pothole.*

*The viewing platform at Pennsylvania's Official State Pothole—*
*don't lean over too far.*

the westbound Schuylkill Expressway. No, Pennsylvania's official state pothole can be found just off Route 6 in Lackawanna County between Scranton and Carbondale in the borough of Archbald. It is the only pothole to have a state park named after it.

But this is no ordinary pothole—it's a glacial pothole. During the ice age, glacial meltwater carrying sand and gravel and rock particles fell like a waterfall hundreds of feet through crevasses in the Laurentide Continental Glacier, forming a pothole in the bedrock beneath. When the glacier finally receded, trees and other vegetation grew on top of it so that you'd never know there was a pothole there in the first place—sort of like nature's asphalt.

The Archbald Pothole would have remained hidden from humans forever, perhaps, if it hadn't been situated in the most heavily mined anthracite region in Northeast Pennsylvania. In 1884 a coal miner named Patrick Mahon set off an explosive charge while extending a tunnel, when suddenly tons of water and rock came tumbling down, setting off a panic in the mine. After removing between 800 and 1,000 tons of stones rubbed round by the glacier, mine inspectors discovered that the miner had opened up the bottom of a pothole about 38 feet from the surface.

In 1887 a fence was built around the perimeter of the pothole and the walls were shored up to prevent collapse as the fame of the pothole spread throughout the geological community, which dubbed Archbald as "a world-class glacial pothole." In 1914 the widow of the landowner turned over a one-acre plot containing the pothole to the Lackawanna Historical Society. In 1940 the county added 150 acres to the site as a park, and later turned the site over to the state of Pennsylvania. The Archbald Pothole State Park was officially dedicated in 1964.

Today the Archbald Pothole is a major tourist attraction, unlike the Schuylkill Expressway westbound pothole, the Route 611 southbound pothole, and the Route 309 northbound pothole, all of which continue to attract a fair share of motorist attention because, unlike Archbald, these potholes are actually getting bigger.

## FIRE IN THE HOLE
### Centralia

It started, some say, as a trash fire in a landfill located in one of the abandoned coal mines that honeycomb this valley between Big Mountain and Mahanoy Mountain on the edge of Pennsylvania's Western-Middle anthracite field. It was Memorial Day weekend in 1962 when the fire underground was first noticed. It's been burning ever since, like a subterranean forest fire with an inexhaustible supply of fuel. The town above, Centralia, has become a symbol of mankind's futile efforts to bandage the wounds the earth has suffered to serve humanity's needs and greed.

In its heyday, Centralia was never much of a town, except for the people who called it home. It sat isolated at the end of a lonely stretch of Route 42 through Colombia County. Its nearest neighbors were Ashland in Schuylkill County and Mt. Carmel in Northumberland County. The only reason you would have heard of Centralia, if you've heard of it at all, is because it's been on fire since John F. Kennedy was President.

A visit to Centralia is a visit to a ghost town. There is no town, so to speak. Most of the commercial buildings, including churches, have been leveled. What remains are scattered homes populated by people too ornery or too proud or too hopeless to leave. At first, the state and the federal government tried to fight the fire by depriving it of oxygen. But the fire was too resourceful, the earth too seamed with cracks as well as veins of combustible coal. Deadly gases began seeping into basements. People got sick. The government tried to vent the gases, but the fire kept moving, silently, inexorably, to new areas.

Finally, the government began condemning properties and paying to relocate people. According to the Pennsylvania Department of Environmental Protection, close to $40 million has been spent fighting the spread of the fire and paying Centralians to move. There were 1,100 people who called Centralia home in 1962. By the year 2000 the number was fewer than twenty. There's no longer a post office in Centralia. The only public building listed in the phone book is the Centralia Fire Department (570–875–0687), but if you call, don't be surprised if there is no answer.

Centralia is not easy to get to and harder to find once you're almost there. Traffic is redirected off Route 61 between Ashland and Mt. Carmel. The town is not officially off-limits, but there are signs warning of noxious gases. It's not a tourist attraction, but it is a sad Pennsylvania curiosity.

## WHERE THE TONGUES FORKED
### Easton

E aston was the scene of two thoroughly despicable treaties negotiated with the Native American Lenni Lenape tribes and the English colonists. In fact, the expression "white man speaks with forked tongue" could well have originated in the Easton treaty known as the Walking Purchase. William Penn was an honorable man in his dealings with the natives, but when he returned to England and turned over the administration to his son, Thomas, the Penn name was tarnished. In 1737 Thomas Penn produced a "lost" treaty negotiated by his father with the Delaware tribe for as much land as a man could walk off in a day and a half. The Indians under Chief Lappowinsoe were leery about the legitimacy of the document but, they reasoned, how much land can a man walk off in thirty-six hours?

What Chief Lappowinsoe didn't know was that the Penns had cleared a trail through the wilderness before the day of the walk, which started from Wrightstown in Bucks County. Not only that, but three of the fastest runners in the colony had been hired to pace off the land in a relay team. By the end of the day-and-a-half "walk" the runners had traveled more than 50 miles and the land within totaled 1,200 square miles, an area almost the size of Rhode Island, which includes most of Pike, Monroe, Lehigh, and Northhampton Counties. The Indians knew they had been robbed. Chief Lappowinsoe complained that the white men "should have walked a few miles and then sat down and smoked a pipe, and now and then have shot a squirrel, and not have kept up the Run, Run all day." But he felt honor bound to abide by the treaty, which was the beginning of the Delaware's westward migration that eventually took them as far as Oklahoma.

The next Easton treaty took place in 1757, following a
period of open warfare on the settlers by the Delawares, who by
then were clearly aware of how hugely they had been swindled.
This time the negotiations were handled by Chief Teedyuscung,
and the dirty trick played by the colonial negotiators was to ply
the chief with firewater. "It must shock you to hear that pains
have been made to make the King [Teedyuscung] drunk every
night since the business began," wrote Charles Thomson, a
twenty-eight-year-old schoolteacher from Philadelphia who
acted as Chief Teedyuscung's personal secretary during the
treaty negotiations. "On Saturday, under pretense of rejoicing
for the victory gained by the King of Prussia, and the arrival of
the fleet, a bonfire was ordered to be made and liquor given to
the Indians to induce them to dance," Thomson wrote to a
friend. "For fear they should get sober on Sunday and be fit the
next day to enter on business, under pretense that the
Mohawks had requested it, another bonfire was ordered to be
made and more liquor given them."

With Thomson watching his back, Teedyuscung was not
swindled in that treaty. Thomson faithfully recorded the chief's
words and in gratitude he was given the Lenni Lenape name
*Wegh-Wu-Law-Mo-End,* which meant Man Who Talks the Truth.
"It's as true as if Charles Thomson's name is on it" became a
popular expression throughout the United States until the Revolutionary period.

## THE FRENCH CONNECTION
### French Azilum

If Marie Antoinette had only said, "You've got a friend in
Pennsylvania" instead of "Let them eat cake," who knows
what would have happened in Bradford County? If the deposed
queen of France had made it to the refuge prepared for her and

*Marie Antionette never lived to see it, but this is the view from the
Marie Antionette Scenic view of French Azilum on the far side of the
Susquehanna River in Bradford County.*

other French nobles in Pennsylvania, perhaps the village of
French Azilum would have been called "Paris on the Susque-
hanna." French loyalists arrived in northeastern Pennsylvania
in the fall of 1793 to settle the village on the shores of the
Susquehanna about 10 miles south of Towanda. As it was,
Marie Antoinette and King Louis XVI lost their heads during
the French Revolution before they could join other fleeing
French nobility in America.

The settlers were assisted in their venture by wealthy
Philadelphians Robert Morris and French-born Stephen Girard,
and the village of Azilum was laid out in a gridiron pattern

with 413 half-acre plots surrounding a two-acre market square. By the following spring, thirty rough log cabin structures had been erected by French settlers, many of them refugees from the slave revolt on the island of Santo Domingo (Haiti). The largest of the structures was La Grande Maison, a massive two-story log structure measuring 80 by 60 feet with numerous small windows and eight fireplaces. This was supposed to have been the deposed queen's residence, but after her execution it was used as a public hall where visiting French dignitaries such as the devious foreign minister Tallyrand and the future French king Louis Phillipe were entertained.

Following the Reign of Terror and the normalization of the domestic situation in France and Haiti, many of the French loyalists, unused to the rough life of frontier America, returned home or to the Caribbean or to established southern cities such as Charleston and New Orleans. That, combined with the bankruptcy of American patron Robert Morris and the invitation by Napoleon Bonaparte for the return of French exiles, led to the end of Azilum as a functioning French town in Pennsylvania by 1803. There were fifty buildings left behind, including several small shops, a schoolhouse, a theater, and a chapel. None of the original structures remains, although a reconstruction of a 1790s log cabin is on the town's site, as well as the lovely whitewashed LaPorte house, built in 1836 by the son of one of the original French settlers. The French influence did not vanish completely from Northeastern Pennsylvania following the failure of the Azilum colony. Among the French refugee families who remained to settle in the area are the LaPortes, Homets, LeFevres, Brevosts, and D'Autremonts, none of whom at last sighting, have lost their heads.

The French Azilum Historic Site is now operated by the Pennsylvania Museum and Historical Commission, but the vista of what the area looks like can be seen from the Marie Antoinette Lookout on Route 6 on the east side of the Susquehanna River near Standing Stone Road. (French Azilum, R.R. 2, Box 266, Towanda, Pennsylvania, 18848. Call 570–265–3376.)

# THE HANDPRINT ON THE PRISON WALL
## Jim Thorpe

Sure, I knew the Irish had it rough, I knew they were exploited by the coal mines, I knew the company store owned their bodies and souls. But until I saw the gallows with the four ropes and the handprint on the prison wall, I guess I never saw how rough.

Midway up the hill on West Broadway in picturesque Jim Thorpe—The Switzerland of Pennsylvania, according to the welcoming signs—is the Old Jail Museum, formerly the Carbon County Prison, built in 1871 and designed by Edward Haviland, whose famous father gave us and the world the first state penitentiary on Fairmount Avenue in Philadelphia. It was here on June 21, 1877, that four so-called Molly Maguires were strangled to death (one took seventeen minutes to die) from the same scaffold after a shameful trial orchestrated by the president of the Philadelphia & Reading Railroad and prosecuted by his private attorneys based on evidence provided by his private police force.

Twenty Mollies in all would hang. They were Irish immigrants guilty of protesting conditions in the coal mines, where a man could earn forty-nine cents for mining a ton of coal and receive a bill for supplies at the end of the day. "Bobtail checks" they called them. Tons loaded minus supplies provided equaled $0.00. Then in 1875 they cut the miners' pay by ten percent.

After surviving a seven-month strike, the owners rewarded the returning miners by cutting their pay another ten percent. Desperate men do desperate things. There were murders on both sides. Only the Mollies met the gallows.

On the wall of Cell No. 17 of the Old Jail, like a modern-day Shroud of Turin, is a handprint said to belong to one of the Mollies before his execution. He rubbed his hand on the dirt of

*Cell No. 17 of the Old Jail, where the handprint of a miner unjustly sent to*
*his death over a hundred years ago can still be seen on the cell wall.*

the floor and held it against the wall until the four fingers and
the thumb were clearly outlined. It will remain for the next
century, he told his guards in 1877, as a symbol of injustice.
They shrugged their shoulders and got on with the business of
death. Afterward, they returned to the cell and tried to wash
the handprint off the wall, but it wouldn't come off. They wiped
it and washed it. Then they painted over it. Then they dug out
the plaster and replastered the spot. But always the handprint
returned, as real as conscience and just as inexplicable.

  In 1975 the *National Enquirer* hired a college professor to
perform a spectographic analysis of the handprint to determine
its origin and what it consisted of. The professor's report indicated that there was nothing there. No grime, no perspiration,
no pigmentation, no nothing. According to the analysis the
handprint doesn't exist. But it's there.

  The Old Jail Museum itself is open for tours only on week-
ends. In the dungeon I visited beneath the prison, there was no

*Even the National Enquirer can't explain this mysterious handprint.*

electricity and only one toilet in sixteen cells used for solitary confinement. Others used buckets emptied only when the prisoner was released. The most startling aspect about the tour is the realization that people were actually serving time here until recent years. The cells for solitary confinement were used until 1980, and the prison remained open until 1995. (Old Jail Museum; call 570–325–5259.)

# HOW JIM THORPE CAME TO PENNSYLVANIA

*In the light of day on a September afternoon the town of Jim Thorpe glows with a rust red from the Carbon County courthouse. The building was built with stone quarried from the mountain called Mauch Chunk ("Bear Mountain" to the original inhabitants, who called themselves Lenni Lenape, which in their tongue meant "original inhabitants"). The town itself was called Mauch Chunk until 1954, when the body of the greatest American athlete, Jim Thorpe, was interred there in exchange for its original name.*

*No small irony there—an Indian name changed to honor an Indian with a European name. On May 28, 1888, in what was still called Indian Territory, now called Oklahoma, a nine-and-a-half-pound baby boy was born to a member of the Thunder Clan of the Sac and Fox tribe. He was born at sunrise. His mother named him Wa-tho-huck, meaning "Bright Path." His father, Hiram Thorpe, a direct descendent of Chief Black Hawk and an accomplished athlete in every sport he endeavored, named his son James.*

*The story of Jim Thorpe, All-American, is better known to most people through the movie by that name, starring Burt Lancaster. But Jim Thorpe was a real person and his athletic exploits led him to be named the best athlete of the first half of the twentieth century in a poll by sportswriters in 1950. Thorpe broke into the American consciousness in 1907 when he came to Pennsylvania's famous Carlisle Indian Institute and made it even more famous by playing football under the coach who would himself become a legend, Glenn "Pop" Warner. Playing in a game against national football power Army, Thorpe scored on the opening kickoff, which was called back due to a penalty. On the ensuing kickoff, Thorpe ran for another touchdown on Carlisle's way to a 27–6 victory. "He was able to do everything anyone else could do but he could do it better," said Army cadet Dwight D. Eisenhower, who Thorpe put out of the game with a crushing*

*Final resting place for "the greatest athelete in the world."*

tackle that ended Ike's football career. "There was no one like him in the world."

In 1912, Thorpe won two gold medals at the Stockholm Olympics in the decathlon and pentathlon. He met King Gustav V of Sweden, who shook Thorpe's hand and said, "You, sir, are the greatest athlete in the world." That is the quote that appears on Jim Thorpe's tomb, located a couple of miles outside of downtown Jim Thorpe on North Street (Route 903). Thorpe played professional baseball for the Giants, Reds, and Braves. He was the highest-paid player in the National Football League, of which he served as president from 1920 until 1926. He could do everything on a football field, including kick. On a return to Carlisle in 1941 at the age of 52, Thorpe stood in the middle of the field and drop-kicked a football over the goal. He then turned and placekicked a field goal over the other end zone—wearing street shoes.

When he died in 1953, a newspaper editor in Carbon County seized upon the idea of bringing Jim Thorpe's body to the towns of Mauch Chunk and East Mauch Chunk, which would merge and change their names to Jim Thorpe. Thorpe's widow agreed to move his body to Pennsylvania, and in 1954, one hundred years after the founding of East Mauch Chunk, the athlete's body was buried there. The Jim Thorpe Memorial has been augmented in recent years with a sculpture garden and metal placards telling stories from his life.

## LITTLE BEAR WOMAN
### Mocanaqua

Just downstream from the borough of Shickshinny in
Luzerene County, on the east side of the Susquehannah
River directly across from Dogtown, lies the tiny village of
Mocanaqua, the Indian name for the most famous Pennsylvanian
you've never heard of. Her name was Frances Slocum, and she
was among the ill-fated clan of Connecticut Yankees that settled
in the Wyoming Valley of northeastern Pennsylvania in the
1760s. (In fact, what is now the city of Scranton was called
Slocum's Hollow.) The family found themselves the lightning
rods of hostility from Indians, British redcoats, and especially
native Pennsylvanians who thought that the colonists from the
Nutmeg State were nuts to come all the way from New England
and declare this area part of Connecticut. This led to the Yankee-
Pennamite Wars, which were interrupted by the Revolutionary
War, which in this part of Pennsylvania is remembered forever
for a disastrous engagement between the American garrison at
Forty Fort and the combined British-Indian forces that became
known as the Wyoming Massacre.

Jonathan and Ruth Slocum were Quaker farmers, nonvio-
lent and fair minded, who had a good relationship with the
native tribes of the area. Even after the Wyoming Massacre in
July 1778, in which upwards of 300 men, women, and children
were slaughtered by the Indian allies of the British, the Slocum
family felt secure in their homestead in what is now Wilkes-
Barre. In the middle of a November day in 1778, while the
adults and older siblings of the Slocum clan were off working
in distant parts of the farm, a raiding party of three Delaware
Indians entered the Slocum cabin and made off with five-year-
old Frances, leaving a brother and sister behind.

Frances Slocum was never seen again. At least not for almost fifty years. In 1835, a fur trader by the name of George W. Ewing was doing business with the Miami tribe near Fort Wayne, Indiana, when he noticed an old woman with white features. In her native Miami tongue, he asked her questions and learned that she was born white, the child of Quakers in Pennsylvania named Slocum. Since being taken from her home by the Delawares she had lived with the Miamis, raised by a loving father and mother who had lost their daughter of about the same age. They named her Mocanaqua, which means "little bear woman." She married twice; her second husband, Shepoconah, became a powerful chief among the Miamis. They had children and moved to Indiana with the tribe.

Touched by her story, Ewing wrote a letter to the postmaster in Lancaster, Pennsylvania, telling the tale and asking him to publicize the story, seeking to find surviving members of the Slocum family. Two years later, Frances Slocum was reunited with her younger brother and sister, who had never lost hope of finding her. She chose to remain with her family of fifty years, but a few years later she used her status as a white woman and Indian mother to establish legitimacy for the claims of the Miamis to land in Indiana. Her story, "The Lost Child of Wyoming," had become famous. In a treaty signed by President Zachary Taylor in 1838, the land occupied by the Miamis in Indiana was granted (temporarily) to the tribe because of the claim by Frances Slocum's Indian-fathered daughter, Ozahsinqua. Among white Americans, Frances Slocum became known as "White Rose of the Miamis" and upon her death in 1847 a monument was built along the Mississinewa River in Indiana.

In Pennsylvania, her name lives on the banks of the Susquehanna River as a town named Mocanaqua, "little bear woman." For the Native American language–impaired there is also the 1,035-acre Frances Slocum State Park, 10 miles northwest of her Wilkes-Barre birthplace.

# WHY, OH WHY, WYOMING?

*T*he state of Wyoming is named after Pennsylvania's
Wyoming Valley. Why, one would wonder, would a
territory carved out of the then-territories of Dakota,
Utah, and Idaho in 1868, and eventually granted state-
hood in 1890, be named for a relatively unknown valley
2,000 miles away? All of those territorial names were
Indian in origin, but Wyoming is an eastern American
Indian name, the language equivalent of giving a
French province a Russian name. In Algonquin, the
word wyoming means either "large prairie place" or
"mountains and valleys alternating" depending on
whether you are using the French translation or the
Russian.

The name Wyoming was famous in nineteenth-century America because of an eighteenth-century American massacre made more lyrical, if not more famous,
by a Scottish poet named Thomas Campbell. In 1809
Campbell wrote an epic poem, "Gertrude of Wyoming,"
about a Revolutionary War battle on Pennsylvania soil
that, I'm sure, most Pennsylvanians have never heard
of. (I base that on the fact that I had never heard of it,
and I'm the Pennsylvania guy writing this book.) In the
1800s, Gertrude of Wyoming was as famous a name as
Monica Lewinsky and for pretty much the same reasons—she was a famous victim everyone knew about,
and nobody wanted to be in her shoes—although more
people admired Gertrude. She was the fictional heroine
of a horrific ordeal. During the Revolutionary War, the
Wyoming Massacre outside Wilkes-Barre was the
British equivalent of the My Lai Massacre during the
war in Vietnam.

On July 3, 1778, a force of 400 keen but poorly
trained Pennsylvania citizen militia, most too young or
too old to be proper soldiers, advanced under General
Zebulon Butler from a fortified position to meet the
forces of British General John Butler, a distant relative,
and his Iroquois allies under Chief Sayenqueraghta. It
was a scene out of a movie. Think of the massacre of
the British and Americans by the Indians in the Daniel
Day Lewis version of Last of the Mohicans.

The continentals were drawn into a trap. While
advancing on a line of apparently retreating British
soldiers after a brief engagement, the Americans were
attacked on both flanks by hundreds of Iroquois warriors crouching in the high grass. The untrained
farmer soldiers panicked. Some fought. Some ran. They
all died. Men were roasted alive in sight of the American fort where the remaining garrison huddled with the
women and children. At midnight under firelight, a old
white woman, who had been captured by the Iroquois
as a child and later married to a chief, walked in a circle and personally executed between sixteen and twenty
American soldiers with a tomahawk. She was known as
Queen Esther and said to be the daughter of a French-
man named Montour, as in Montour County.

When the soldiers were sacrificed, the Iroquois
turned their attention to the women and children and
remaining men fleeing Forty Fort. Gertrude of
Wyoming was one of them. The event became the story
that became the poem that became the metaphor for
America's brave resistance and eventual triumph over
British tyranny and native American savagery on the
frontier. At least, that was how it was seen in 1868
when Wyoming got its name. But then again, consider
the options. Would you want to live in a state named
Gertrude?

## THE BLONDE BOMBSHELL
### Pen Argyl

Jayne Mansfield was a Bryn Mawr girl. Literally. She was born in Bryn Mawr Hospital on April 19, 1933. By the time she died in a late-night car crash on the road from Biloxi, Mississippi, to New Orleans, Louisiana, on June 29, 1967, she'd spent most of her life away from her home state. But she is buried in Fairview Cemetery outside Pen Argyl in Northhampton County, where her mother's family still lives. Jayne Mansfield was the poor man's Norma Jean, a not-quite Marilyn Monroe. She was famous mostly for two things, which she showed off at every opportunity.

Mansfield arrived in Hollywood in the mid-'50s and got her first job after writing "40-22-34" on a card she left in a producer's office. Never a star but always an attraction, Jayne Mansfield once said, "I decided early in life that the first thing to do was to become famous—I'd worry about acting later." Jayne lived up (or down) to her ambitions. While trying to break into the movies, she won a series of beauty contests with names like Miss Negligee, Miss Nylon Sweater, Miss Geiger Counter, and Miss Tomato. She appeared in a legitimate hit movie, *Will Success Spoil Rock Hunter?*, but mostly she is remembered as a heaving bosom in various low-budget foreign movies like *The Loves of Hercules* starring her muscle-man husband, Mickey Hargatay.

In 1964 when the Beatles arrived in the United States on their first tour, they were asked which American celebrity they would most like to meet. The lads chose Jayne Mansfield. Upon meeting them, she asked the mop-topped John Lennon if his hair was real. He replied by looking at her breasts and asking, "Are those real?"

In the end, Jayne Mansfield's career in Hollywood was all
but over. She was appearing at a supper club in Biloxi when
she died in a car crash, in which—contrary to widely held
belief—she was not decapitated. A blonde bouffant wig she was
wearing was thrown from the vehicle, which started the
rumors. Like the swimming pool outside her Sunset Boulevard
home and the bed inside it, Jayne Mansfield's tombstone is in
the shape of a heart. The inscription beneath her name reads,
WE LIVE TO LOVE YOU MORE EACH DAY. (Fairview Cemetery, Middletown Road just outside of Pen Argyl.)

# THE DAY THE EARTH ATE THE RIVER
## Port Griffith

I f Don McLean wrote an epic song about the Pennsylvania
coal industry along the lines of "American Pie," the date January 22, 1959, would be remembered as "the day the music
died." That was the day the earth swallowed the river and old
King Coal drowned.

It happened in Port Griffith, one of the towns "up the line"
as they say in Wilkes-Barre, meaning the Wyoming Valley communities along the Susquehanna River north of it and south of
Scranton, where the same towns become "down the line." There
were eighty-one miners at work that day in the Knox Coal
Company's two mine shafts, one of them a nearly exhausted
dig in the Pittston Vein, which ran alongside and underneath
the Susquehanna River. Soon it became an underground
branch of the Susquehanna. At 11:20 in the morning, the river
broke through the roof of the mine, sending a virtual Niagara
of water into not only the Knox mine but into all the other
mines that honeycombed the valley. Most of the miners
escaped, but twelve were swept away.

The hole in the river formed a giant whirlpool that sucked 2.7 million gallons of water per minute into the mines. Attempts were made to plug the hole with fifty-ton coal cars, called gondolas, that were dumped into the river. Sixty gondolas were sucked into the whirlpool and vanished like toys down the bathtub drain. It took another 400 coal cars plus 25,000 cubic yards of earth, rock, and boulders before the hole in the river stopped gulping after three days. During that time more than 10 billion gallons of water poured into the mines. The Knox Mine Disaster, as it has been known ever since, marked the end of deep anthracite mining in the region. It was Pennsylvania's wreck of *Edmund Fitzgerald,* and like Lake Superior, the Susquehanna never gave up her dead. The bodies of the twelve miners were never found.

In the aftermath, the web of greed and corruption that caused the Knox Mine disaster was uncovered. State mine inspectors turned the other way as Knox Mine officials ordered their miners to dig shafts more than 125 feet past the "stop line" beneath the Susquehanna. When the river burst through, only six feet separated the mine roof from the riverbed. One of the founders of the Knox Mine, John Sciandra, was the boss of the northeastern Pennsylvania organized crime family. A secret partner in the Knox mine was an official with the United Mine Workers Union. The level of corruption by government inspectors, the betrayal by union leaders, and the criminal greed that drove it all were exposed in the trials of ten people indicted in the aftermath of the Knox Mine Disaster. Only three served jail time.

In front of St. Joseph's Church in Port Griffith stands a tombstone engraved with the names of the twelve men who perished in the Knox Mine Disaster. Every January 22 there is a memorial service at the church not only for the twelve dead miners, but also for the death of the coal industry. In the wake of the mine flooding, 7,500 jobs were lost in towns up and down the line.

## H o t   N e w   B e e r   i s   A m e r i c a' s   O l d e s t
### P o t t s v i l l e

O ne of Pennsylvania's most popular beers was an
overnight success, comparatively speaking. A decade or
so must seem like the day before yesterday to a company that's
been brewing beer for more than 170 years. Before there was a
Bud for you or a Schaeffer to sing about, before Miller even
had life, let alone a high life, there was a Yuengling Brewery in
Pottsville. Founded in 1829 by David G. Yuengling, the family-
owned business is America's oldest brewery, and was so designated by the National Registry of Historical Places during the
Bicentennial celebration in 1976.

To have survived all that time, the Yuengling Brewery had
to overcome a hurdle that put most of its competition out of
business for good: the Eighteenth Amendment to the Constitution, better known as Prohibition, which became law in 1919.
Yuengling responded by switching over to the production of an
almost nonalcoholic brew called near beer. In 1920, the company opened a dairy next to the brewery. Somehow, the company survived until 1933 when Prohibition was repealed. To
celebrate the victory of "wets" over "dries" at the polls,
Yuengling produced its first real beer in more than a decade
and called it Winner. (A truckload of Winner beer was shipped
to new President Franklin D. Roosevelt as a welcome to the
White House.)

For most beer drinkers outside of Central Pennsylvania,
Yuengling remained the answer to a trivia question (What is
America's oldest . . . ?) until the fifth generation of Yuenglings
transformed it from a beloved regional beer into nationally
known brand name. Richard L. Yuengling purchased the com-

pany from his father and uncle in 1985 and immediately began marketing the product to younger customers. The result has been a 400 percent increase in sales. Yuengling's Black & Tan— half porter, half lager—was an immediate hit among urban sophisticates in Philadelphia and Baltimore. Soon Yuengling lager had become a staple in bars where just a year before people didn't know how to pronounce it (for the record, it's *YING-ling*). To this day, the order of "lager" will get you a bottle of Yuengling in most bars.

In 1998 Yuengling brewery began the largest expansion in its seventeen-decade history with the construction of a new brewery in Tampa, Florida, of all places. The original brewery at Fifth and Mahantongo Streets in Pottsville is still the greatest, however, and tours are conducted twice a day Monday through Friday and three times a day on Saturday during the summer months. For more information, call 570–622–4141.

### D E E P   B E L O W   S C R A N T O N
#### S c r a n t o n

Tony Donofrio has an upstate Pennsylvania voice that could crack slate, even here, 250 feet underground in the Lackawanna Coal Mine outside Scranton. Tony is our tour guide and his voice does not require amplification. It is a high-pitched, high-speed voice with wide-nasal midwestern *A* sounds, perfect for a bunch of beefy guys sitting around at table in Chicago toasting "Da Bears!" Tony has been a coal miner since 1964, when the coal industry in this part of Pennsylvania was already on its last legs. You can tell he'd rather be digging coal than giving tours, but you can also tell that he

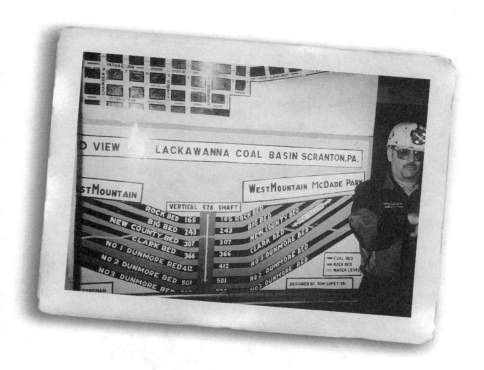

*The story of the Lackawana Coal Mine is the story of Scranton.*

takes pride in giving tours to people who shake their heads at the thought of human beings spending their working lives in perpetual darkness and danger. "It's not for everybody," says Tony of the miner's life; twenty people in the tour group nod.

The tour takes about an hour, more than enough time to convince even hardy souls that working life aboveground has its sweeter pleasures. For instance, there are no monkey veins in most surface jobs. Monkey veins are seams of coal so narrow than miners must crawl on their hands and knees or squat-walk like lesser primates. Assignment to a monkey vein was awarded by the labor union law of natural selection based upon seniority. The more seniority, the less monkey walking. Most of

*That hand sticking up is supposed to be a miner trapped in a cave. Tour guide Tony Donofrio can push a button that makes the hand move, scaring the bejabbers out of visitors to the Lackwanna Coal Mine tour.*

the Lackawanna Coal Mine tour is through roomy and well-lighted chambers, but at some point during the tour, Tony or one of his cohorts will kill the lights just long enough to demonstrate the claustrophobic effects of an optical condition known as pitch black.

"Hear that?" asks Tony, banging an iron rod onto the tunnel roof overhead. "That's solid. That's the sound a miner wants to hear. Now hear this?" he asks, demonstrating the sound a miner doesn't want to hear overhead, a muffled dull *thunk* rather than the solid *ping* of iron on rock. Thunk means something's wrong, a cavity no root canal can fill.

The story of the Lackawanna Coal Mine is the story of Scranton. The city took its current name in 1851 from the founders of the Lackawanna Iron and Coal Co., established in 1840. George W. and Seldon Scranton discovered that the black diamond heat of burning anthracite did wonderful hardening things to nails and, later, rails. The expression "hard as nails" may have been around for a long time, but Scranton made nails harder, stronger. By 1900, one out of six miles of railroad tracks laid in the United States was forged steel from Scranton.

The owners of the region's coal mines felt they were the stewards of God's abundant gifts underground. They were, in their own words, "Christian men to whom God in His infinite wisdom had given control of the property interests in this country!" A young man named Henry Ford wanted to build an automobile manufacturing plant in Scranton, but the coal barons at play in the fields of the lord felt such employment opportunities would only confuse their childlike workers, not to mention cut into profits by creating a competitive wage situation among prospective employees. Ford looked elsewhere, and Scranton looks back in regret, or perhaps relief, that it did not become Pennsylvania's Detroit.

After all, being Pennsylvania's Scranton was difficult enough. In 1897 union-minded miners in Lattimer outside of Hazelton protested wages and conditions and were answered with a hail of bullets from sheriff's deputies that killed nineteen outright and wounded another forty-nine. The Lattimer Massacre led to the rise of a young labor leader named John L. Mitchell, who was elected president of the United Mine Workers union two years later at the age of twenty-nine. Mitchell, whose statue stands in front of the Lackawanna County courthouse in Scranton, led the mine workers in a bitter and passionate and seemingly never-ending strike in 1902. It was the longest strike in labor history until that time—165 days or twenty-three weeks or five-and-a-half months—requiring the personal involvement of President Theodore Roosevelt to settle it. It transformed the labor-management landscape, prompting laws to protect the rights of working men and their families.

The need for such laws is apparent here, 1,200 feet downhill from the opening of the Lackawanna Coal Mine. That's where we meet a child, actually a mannequin of a child, who could be seven years old but looks younger. The little boy is called a nipper. His job was to open and close doors to allow coal cars to pass and ventilation to circulate. "This nipper," said Tony, "had this much light to work with for eight, ten hours a day." Think of a Zippo lighter illuminating a subway concourse. That's how much light his coal oil headlamp could muster. Even by 1908, four years after the strike, one out of four mine workers was a boy between the ages of seven and sixteen.

The skies above Scranton foundries glowed twenty-four hours a day until the Pennsylvania iron ore gave out. Coal was king for another generation, but peak production came in 1917 during the first World War. Nothing has been the same since the Knox Mine Disaster of 1958. But one thing is true in Scranton, Wilkes-Barre, Hazelton, Shamokin, and wherever else God's self-appointed chosen stewards harvested the wealth below the earth—childhood is no longer as dark as it once was. (Lackawanna Coal Mine is open daily 10:00 A.M. to 4:30 P.M. April through November.)

# NAME GAMES:

## THE GOOD, THE BAD, AND THE UGLY

*How would you like to grow up in a town called Drab?
Or Drain Lick? Or Grimesville? All these are actual names of
towns in Pennsylvania. So are Brave and Paradise and
Fearnot. Pennsylvania is as full of town names that
inspire—Independence, Challenge, Enterprise, Freedom,
Energy—as it is town names that, well, don't inspire: Bland-
burg, Needmore, Slabtown, Slate Lick, Burnt Cabins, Scalp
Level, Spraggs. For every Prosperity, there is a Grindstone.
For every Hearts Content, there is an Ickesburg. For every
Friendsville, there is a Lickingville. For every Crown, there is
a Crumb.*

*Pennsylvania is rich in names like Diamond, Chrome,
Gold, and Pearl. It is also saddled with town names like
Hungry Hollow, Gravel Lick, Rife, and Seldom Seen. There's
Savage, Rough and Ready, Stalker, and Thumptown. There's
Shaft and Taxville.*

*Pennsylvania has town names that seem to be linked by
emotion, if not geography. Does Desire lead to Panic? Does
Defiance result in Force? Are Fairchance and Fairplay in the
same athletic conference? Are Frugality and Economy the
result of Effort? Do you have to go through Grimville to
find Jollytown? Is Husband a destination for unmarried
women from Hope? Do they Ache when they find their Hero
is with a Lover? Can they Admire him when they find out
she's really from Hooker? Is Progress possible without
Endeavor? Is Decorum compatible with Candor?
It's all something you have to Hunker down
and Muse about, perhaps at one of the Two
Taverns.*

*Pennsylvania has a King and a Queen. It
has a Tippecanoe and a Tyler too. It has a
Forest as well as a Gump. But for some reason the
town of Vim lacks a matching Vigor.*

# THE WAR BETWEEN THE STATES
## Wilkes-Barre

A t about the same time that Charles Mason and Jeremiah
Dixon arrived in Philadelphia to begin the survey that
would settle the boundary dispute between Pennsylvania and
Maryland in 1763, settlers from Connecticut began arriving in
the Wyoming Valley of northeast Pennsylvania. Not only did
they claim that the land belonged to them, they claimed that
the land was part of the colony of Connecticut. Now, it's under-
standable that there could be some rival claims to the same
land by adjoining colonies such as Pennsylvania and Maryland,
especially when there are no natural boundaries like rivers to
mark where one state ends and another begins. But how the
heck do settlers from Connecticut leapfrog over New York, land
in Pennsylvania, and call it home?

Needless to say, there was a king involved. In fact, it was
the same King Charles II who in 1681 granted William Penn
the land in the New World that would become Pennsylvania.
Unfortunately, nineteen years earlier in 1662, King Charles II
had granted portions of northeastern Pennsylvania to the
colony of Connecticut. Like the border dispute with Maryland,
the land feud between Pennsylvania and Connecticut simmered
for almost a century before being resolved. Unlike the dispute
with Maryland, which was settled with the border survey that
became famous as the Mason-Dixon line, the issue of Connecticut Yankees in Pennsylvania was resolved the old-fashioned
way, in a series of bloody but historically obscure battles called
the Yankee-Pennamite Wars.

Pennamite was the biblical-sounding name (think
Philistines) that the proper colonists from Connecticut called
their Pennsylvania neighbors. In 1762 the first Connecticut set-

tlers arrived in the area around Wilkes-Barre. A year later the Yankees were driven out of the region by the Lenni Lenape in a massacre sparked by the murder of their Chief Teedyuscung, which they blamed on the new settlers. When the Yankees returned in 1769, they found that their Pennamite rivals had taken over their lands and built a fort to defend their hold on the land. Thus began the first Yankee-Pennamite War (1769–71).

There were two or three wars, depending on which historian you believe. All agree that the combatants took time out to join forces against the British during the Revolutionary War. Hostilities recommenced after the Continental Congress court of arbitration ruled in 1782 that the Wyoming Valley belonged to Pennsylvania. But the Connecticut settlers wouldn't leave, and in 1784 the Pennamite forces burned the Yankee stronghold of Wilkes-Barre. Connecticut and Vermont sent reinforcements to fight the Pennamites. It was truly a war between the states. What a mess.

The entire issue wasn't settled until 1799, when the Pennsylvania Legislature passed the Compromise Act to settle the claims of Connecticut. In the end the Connecticut influence in Pennsylvania includes the towns of Wilkes-Barre, Plymouth, Kingston, Pittston, Hanover, and Forty Fort (named after the Connecticut plan to establish townships that could support and protect forty families). The Yankee-Pennamite Wars were more like skirmishes between rival militias, and the total casualties numbered in the hundreds rather than thousands, but who knew that Pennsylvania and Connecticut actually fought a war against each other? Pennsylvania won, of course. Otherwise we'd all be speaking Yankee.

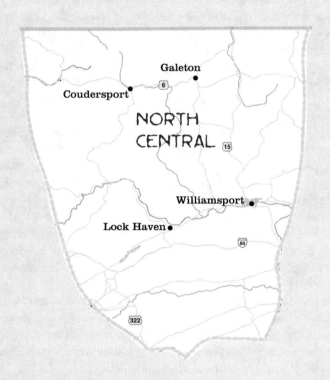

Galeton

Coudersport

NORTH
CENTRAL

Williamsport

Lock Haven

NORTH CENTRAL

# NORTH CENTRAL

## WHEN LUMBER WAS KING
## IN PENNSYLVANIA
### Galeton

It has been written that when William Penn landed in Pennsylvania in 1682, his colony was so thickly forested that a squirrel could run from Philadelphia to Pittsburgh without once setting its feet on the ground. So it's really no leap of imagination to understand how one of Pennsylvania's first and greatest businesses was the lumber industry. Most of the original forest that once carpeted the commonwealth has been cut down at least once. In fact, Pennsylvania's huge state forest system was born in the first half of the twentieth century from lum-

*More deer than people live in sparsely populated Potter County (16,000 people over 1,100 square miles), which calls itself "God's Country."*

*There's an exibit at the Pennsylvania Lumber Museum where dirty old socks hanging from a clothesline to dry add a "scents" of realism to a display about nineteenth-century loggers and how they lived.*

bered-out mountains left barren by the lumber companies that had swept through and moved on in search of more trees. Imagine the leafy rolling mountains we see today throughout central and northern Pennsylvania without a single living tree to bend in the wind.

Much of the growth of mature trees in Pennsylvania is the legacy of Civilian Conservation Corps (CCC), one of the so-called alphabet-soup agencies set up by the federal government during the Great Depression to put millions of unemployed men to work. Between 1933 and 1942 the CCC planted 200 million new trees in the nation's forests, and Pennsylvania has living proof of those efforts. The story of the CCC is among those told at the

Pennsylvania Lumber Museum on Route 6 in Potter County, not
far from Galeton, where one of the largest sawmills in the world
was located when lumber was king in Pennsylvania. The Lumber Museum tells the story of the "woodhicks," the seasonal
lumberjacks who worked from November until April in the lumber camps that dotted the forested landscape of Pennsylvania.

Woodhicks worked from 5:00 A.M. until lights out at 9:00
P.M. six days a week. They lived in bunkhouses in camps of
sixty men and worked through the cold and snow, cutting down
trees and hauling the lumber to train cars traveling on tracks
laid by the lumbermen. It was hard work performed by hard
men who lived in close quarters and rarely bathed. They hung
their wet socks and long johns on clotheslines strung near the
bunkhouse woodstoves and, as the self-guided tour booklet
notes, "The stench of steaming clothes added to body odors is
left to your imagination." Also left to the imagination was the
lumber industry in Pennsylvania, which one hundred years ago
produced the majority of the white pine and hemlock boards
used by builders and cabinet makers in the United States.

For more information, call the museum at (814) 435–2652.

## H O M E   O F   T H E   G R O W L E R
### L o c k   H a v e n

L ock Haven, contrary to popular perception, was not named
because the town's residents leave their doors unlocked.
Even today, that could be said of more Pennsylvania towns
than would care to admit it. Others suggest that Lock Haven
got its name from its founder, Jerry Church, who was a loon
and should have been "locked away" because he lived in a tree
house when everyone else had their feet set firmly on the
ground. This, of course, is a gross exaggeration. Jerry Church
didn't live in a tree house. He had his *law offices* in a tree

*Whatever you do at the Texas Lunch restaurant in*
*Lock Haven, don't order a hoagie.*

house 11 feet off the ground overlooking the Susquehanna
River. He felt it was cheaper than advertising for clients.

Subsequent generations would recognize Jerry Church's
eccentricity for the genius it was. While the rest of Lock Haven
was underwater from regular Susquehanna River floods, Jerry
Church's feet would be dry from his law office perch even during Hurricane Agnes in 1972, after which a dike was built
through downtown.

At any rate, it was Jerry Church, lawyer and land specula-
tor, who founded Lock Haven in 1832, giving it a name that
was bound to attract canal boats operating along the west
branch of the Susquehanna in Clinton County. The canals in

Lock Haven connected the Susquehanna with Bald Eagle Creek. Church had to quit school at the age of fourteen after attempting to kiss his teacher. He worked for two years after that making shingles and then quit, noting in his memoirs that hard work did not agree with him and hurt his feelings.

With Jerry Church as a founder, Lock Haven was bound to have some eccentric institutions, and one of them is Texas Lunch, the all-night diner that is known for growlers the way South Philly is known for hoagies.

The growler, so named because your stomach supposedly growls after eating one, is basically a chili dog with a special recipe. The original Greek owners of the restaurant called their special sandwich a Texas hot dog; they discouraged use of the nickname by charging an extra 25 cents to any customer ordering a growler rather than a Texas hot dog. The current owners have embraced the name, and waitresses wear T-shirts identifying Lock Haven's Texas Lunch as "Home of the Growler." The restaurant is at 204 East Main Street. Call (717) 748-3522.

## LITTLE LEAGUE BASEBALL
### Williamsport

Among Pennsylvania's many exports to the world—a constitutional republic, the Slinky, steel, anthracite, Frankie Avalon, and Crayola crayons—perhaps the most successful has been Little League Baseball. Some 30 million people around the world have played Little League since it was invented in 1939 by a lumberyard clerk from Williamsport, named Carl Stotz. Among them is the current president of the United States, George W. Bush, who played catcher for the Little League team in Midland, Texas. (Al Gore didn't.) Bush is the first president to have played Little League; his father has the distinction of being the first Little League volunteer coach to become president of the United States.

Little League has been a hit around the world since Carl Stotz solicited sponsorship from local businesses to start a youth baseball league. It was Stotz who drew the dimensions of the Little League baseball diamond to be two-thirds the size of the regular baseball field (60 feet from base to base rather than 90, and 40 feet from the pitcher's mound to home plate rather than 60 feet, 6 inches).

In 1939 there were three Little League teams sponsored by Williamsport area companies: Lycoming Dairy, Lundy Lumber, and Jumbo Pretzel. By 1999, the game invented in a Susquehanna River town was being played in Burkina-Faso, an African country with a population less than Pennsylvania's, and the one-hundredth nation to join the Little League. Today there are more than 20,000 Little League programs operating worldwide.

The original home of Little League stands on West Fourth Street in Williamsport, across the street from the Pittsburgh Pirates' minor league baseball club, The Crosscutters, named in honor of Williamsport's famed history in the state's lumber industry. It was on this field that the first twelve Little League World Series were played, from 1947 through 1958.

Since then the World Series has been played across the river in the Howard J. Lamade Stadium in South Williamsport, adjacent to the Peter J. McGovern Little League Museum. Carl Stotz, the founder and first commissioner, was forced out of his position in 1956 when he filed suit in federal court seeking to prevent the expansion of the league. Clearly, he never envisioned the worldwide organization nor the live network TV coverage of the Little League World Series that has accompanied the championship game since 1960.

The main room on the first floor of the Little League museum resembles a baseball playing field, complete with white baselines painted on the floor and a home plate with a man-

*Williamsport, Pennsylvania, the birthplace of Little League Baseball—one of the state's most successful exports.*

nequin catcher and umpire standing behind it. The room literally shrieks "Play ball!" but a sign at the front door advises visitors, NO BATS OR GLOVES ALLOWED IN THE MUSEUM. The exhibits behind glass show every Little League World Series Championship team photo since 1947. That year's Williamsport all-star team wore mismatched uniforms from a local VFW, Sears, Hossers, and 40 & 8 business sponsors. The 1948 Champions from nearby Lock Haven all wore uniforms sponsored by Keds. In 1957 Monterrey, Mexico, became the first of several foreign teams to win the Little League World Series, and the first team to repeat the following year.

*These natural gas-fueled street lamps burn twenty-four hours a day*
*in Wellsboro, the Tioga County seat.*

The Little League Hall of Excellence is a separate room
showing large photographs of Little League alumni who have
gone on to make a name for themselves in sports and other
endeavors. They include major league All-Stars Mike Schmidt
and Tom Seaver, NBA star and U.S. Senator Bill Bradley, movie
star Tom Selleck, author and columnist George Will, and
humorist Dave Barry (I am not making that up).

While I was visiting South Williamsport, construction was
under way for an expansion of the stadium complex (41,200
people crowded into Lamade Stadium to see the 1998 championship game won by Toms River, New Jersey, over Kashima,
Japan). If you make it to see the Little League August Classic,
make sure to take a trip across the Susquehanna River to West
Fourth Street in Williamsport to see the little field where Carl
Stotz started it all.

# THE MILLIONAIRES OF WILLIAMSPORT

The mascot of my alma mater, Lower Merion High School, is a bulldog. I suppose that had something to do with tenaciousness and "Grrrrr" and all that, but as far as I know, Lower Merion Township wasn't infested with bulldogs at any key period in its development. The same cannot be said of Williamsport and millionaires. At one time in the mid-1800s, Williamsport was home to more millionaires per capita than any other town in the United States. The wealth was literally flowing down the Susquehanna River from the lumber trade born of the thick forests of Central Pennsylvania. I have visited other Pennsylvania towns that make the same millionaires-per-capita claim, specifically Jim Thorpe (then Mauch Chunk), but only Williamsport has institutionalized the title by naming its high school teams "The Millionaires."

As you might imagine, a Millionaire mascot should look like a millionaire, and Williamsport's does. Think of the guy on the Monopoly box when he was fifteen years old. No need for a monocle, but decked out in top hat, white gloves, and cane. Perhaps a black cape on a windy day.

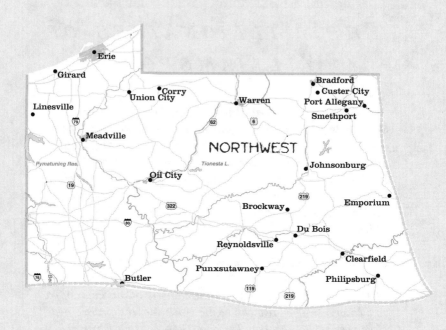

Erie

Girard

Linesville

Corry

Union City

Warren

Bradford

Custer City

Port Allegany

Smethport

79

Meadville

NORTHWEST

Pymatuning Res.

62

6

Tionesta L.

Johnsonburg

Oil City

19

219

Emporium

322

Brockway

Du Bois

80

Reynoldsville

Clearfield

Punxsutawney

Philipsburg

76

Butler

119

219

NORTHWEST

# NORTHWEST

## COLD TOWN, WARM HEART
### Bradford

I t's August and the heater is turned on in the house where
I'm writing this. The heat is always on here—January or
July, it makes no difference—because as hot as it can get
during the day, it can get colder than you'd imagine here at
night.

"Here" is upstate Pennsylvania. It's so upstate that New
York is closer than New Jersey. Buffalo is closer than Pittsburgh. Canada is closer than a foreign country has a right to
be. I am not so much in the middle of nowhere, as on the edge
of nowhere.

"Nowhere" would be the next biggest town, Bradford. I am
on the edge of Bradford, in the village of Lewis Run in McKean
County. Bradford (COLD TOWN, WARM HEARTS reads the sign on
the side of an oil refinery tank in the middle of town) has the
shivering distinction of being the coldest place in the state.
"The Icebox of Pennsylvania," Bradford has been called, a title
shared with neighboring upstate towns of Kane and St. Mary's,
each of which claims to be colder than the other. Lewis Run
runs even cooler.

This I am told inside the Lewis Run home of L. A. "Larry"
Rotheraine, a Philadelphia boy gone country.

There aren't many people where Rotheraine lives now. What
there are are mountains, lots and lots of mountains, those
rolling green Pennsylvania tree humps that rise and fall end-
lessly in these parts and much of the rest of the state. But for

*Cold enough for you?*
*Welcome to "The Icebox*
*of Pennsylvania,"*
*Bradford, where frost*
*can come as early as*
*August.*

whatever reason, the mountains in McKean County and the prevailing winds from the northwest create uniquely cooler atmospheric conditions. Already the leaves are turning on some trees. "Seven years ago year our first frost came on August 21," Rotheraine said.

Rotheraine watches for frost the way a card counter watches for face cards in Atlantic City. That's because the big-city boy gone country is the most successful gardener in McKean County and perhaps in the state of Pennsylvania.

For the last eleven years Rotheraine has been the master gardener at Evergreen Elm, a group home for mentally challenged adults in Bradford, where Rotheraine supervises his clients as they help him work a garden covering a mere two-thirds of an acre. On Saturday night I watched as Rotheraine and three of his clients collected their prize-winning vegetables on the last day of the weeklong McKean County Fair.

"Who's got their long johns on?" asked the radio personality introducing the featured country-western band on the main stage, while Rotheraine and his charges toured the midway on a night when temperatures would drop into the low forties. If McKean County is the icebox of Pennsylvania, then

Rotheraine's garden is the vegetable bin. This year Evergreen Elm gardeners entered thirty different vegetables and won thirty ribbons—twenty-two blue, five red, and three white—at the McKean County Fair. They've been virtually sweeping the top prizes at the fair for the last ten years. In fact, Evergreen Elm decided to limit its entries to thirty just so someone else could get a chance to win the blue. "Our best year was 1995

## THE MOST FAMOUS TOWN THAT DOESN'T EXIST

*Since the international success of the movie* Saving Private Ryan, *Pennsylvania has become a symbol of the home of the citizen soldier. Who can forget the final scene of a now old and gray James Francis Ryan standing at attention and saluting in front of a white cross at the American military cemetery in Normandy? The camera then pushes in to show the name on the cross,* CAPT. JOHN MILLER, PENNSYLVANIA.

*In the movie the American soldiers under his command have bets on what Captain Miller (played by Tom Hanks) did in civilian life and where he lived. In one of the most gripping scenes in the movie, he reveals that he's an English teacher at Thomas Alva Edison High School in Addley, Pennsylvania.*

*In fact, there is no Addley, Pennsylvania. It was a name made up by* Saving Private Ryan *screenwriter Robert Rodat, who grew up in New Hampshire.*

*Master gardener Larry Rotheraine standing next to one of his remarkable cherry tomato plants that yield 2,000 tomatoes per season.*

when we won twenty-seven blue ribbons out of thirty-four entries," Rotheraine said.

What's Rotheraine's secret? It's called Biodynamic Gardening, a compost-intensive process pioneered by the influencial and controversial scientist-writer Dr. Rudolf Steiner (1861–1925), whose spiritualistic concepts of planting and growing vegetables sound like voodoo to traditional agriculturalists. But the proof is in the ribbons and in the yield. Rotheraine's garden produces three to four times the average yield for onions, cabbages, beets, carrots, peppers, squash, and other vegetables. His cherry tomatoes can yield as much as forty times the average; a single plant can grow to 15 feet and produce 2,000 tomatoes a year.

Just imagine what he could do in a warmer climate where the frost won't hit the pumpkins until Halloween. "I could grow more in a warmer climate, but I couldn't get the quality of seeds I get from this cold," Rotheraine said. "Besides, I love it here. This is my home now. These people are my family."

For L. A. Rotheraine, home is where the heat isn't.

# ZIPPO DEE DOO DAH
### Bradford

A t one time or another in your life, you've probably owned a
Zippo lighter. Your Zippo may have had a design, decoration, commemorative decal, or advertisement on the front of it
(mine has gears and the Harley-Davidson Motorcycles logo),
but I guarantee that yours had the same thing written on the
bottom as mine does: Zippo, Bradford, Pa.

Bradford has been
the home to Zippo
lighters since the
beginning, and the
beginning was a summer night in 1932
during a dinner
dance at the Bradford Country Club
where well-to-do
Bradfordians, most
of who were in the
oil business, gathered to complain
about business during those darkest early
days of the Great Depression.

*Even the street lights look like Zippo lighters in Bradford.*

A forty-seven-year-old oilman named George Blaisdell had
almost been wiped out by falling crude oil prices, and to escape
the depressing talk he stepped out onto the balcony for a
smoke. There stood Dick Dresser, an elegantly dressed young

*At the famous Zippo Clinic,
you can see the many ways
Zippo lighters have been,
accidentally, and not so
accidentally, mangled.
There's also a display
showing all the ways Zippo
lighters have been used to
blow up buildings in
Hollywood movies.*

man from a wealthy family, trying to light his cigarette with
some kind of a cheap-looking foreign lighter. When the little
wheel on the top of the lighter struck the flint and sparked the
wick into flame, a lightbulb went on in Blaisdell's head. What if
he could manufacture a better windproof lighter that could be
used in one hand? Zippo dee doo dah!

The first Zippo lighters were boxier in shape, a half inch taller and a quarter inch wider than current models, but that's about the only difference. In the first month, Blaisdell's company produced eighty-two units designed to sell for $1.95 each. Total sales that first month were $69.15. Blaisdell needed something else, something unique to attract attention to his product. He came up with what he called a "forever guarantee," a lifetime replacement or repair warranty that continues to this day.

Today you can view returned Zippo lighters being received and repaired and shipped off by the virtually all-female crew of employees at the Zippo Repair Clinic at the Zippo Lighter Museum in Bradford. One display case at the museum contains a variety of mangled lighters that have been returned over the years. The list of the causes beneath the damaged lighters includes garbage disposal, bulldozer, power mower, ice crusher, and cocker spaniel.

To get to the Zippo museum, visitors must first walk through the Zippo gift shop, where lighters that once cost $1.95 now retail for $35.95. There are Zippos with World Wrestling Federation stars like Stone Cold Steve Austin and The Undertaker. There are Jeep, Ford, and Chevy Zippos. There are Elvis, Beatles, and Kiss Zippos. There's even a *Titanic* Zippo, one of thousands of specialty collectible models manufactured over the years. Outside the Zippo Visitors Center, the streetlights in the parking area and along Zippo Drive are shaped like flaming Zippo lighters.

Incidentally, Blaisdell, who died in 1978 at the age of ninety-three, chose the name Zippo because he was delighted by the sound of a new invention by another Pennsylvania manufacturing company. The Talon Company had revolutionized the clothing industry with a new type of easy-to-use-with-one-hand metal fastener. They called it the zipper. (For more information, call the Zippo Visitors Information Center at 814–368–2700.)

## OIL'S WELL THAT ENDS WELL
### Custer City

The question was worth $125,000. "In what state was the first oil well drilled?" asked Regis Philbin. "(A) California, (B) Oklahoma, (C) Pennsylvania, or (D) Texas." The contestant on *Who Wants to Be a Millionaire* used one of his lifelines, a call to a friend, to be sure of the answer that anyone from Oil City to Wellsboro could come up with in a heartbeat. It was up in Titusville in Crawford County that Colonel Edwin Drake discovered oil on August 27, 1859, by drilling a well 69 feet into the ground that produced twenty barrels of crude oil a day. It was the first time that oil had been obtained in substantial quantities, and it set off a mad rush of drilling and speculating that turned Oil Creek into "The Valley That Changed the World." The Pennsylvania oil rush was *Who Wants to Be a Millionaire* for keeps, but Drake went broke due to competition and falling oil prices. When he made his discovery, oil was selling for $20 a barrel. By 1861 you could buy a barrel of oil for a dime.

This didn't slow oil production in Pennsylvania. After oil was discovered in Bradford in McKean County in 1872 at the imposing depth of 1,200 feet, the greatest oil field in American history went into operation. The Bradford Oil District included all of McKean County and part of neighboring Cattaraugus County, New York. In 1878, the Bradford field produced 6.5 million barrels of oil, 42 percent of the total oil production in the United States. By 1883, Bradford was producing 23 million barrels of oil each year, an incredible 83 percent of American oil production.

Not only was Pennsylvania crude oil plentiful, it was special. The "miracle molecule" found only in Pennsylvania Grade crude oil makes it the best lubricating oil in the world. Unlike asphalt-based oil found everywhere from Texas to Saudi Arabia, Penn-

There are 90,000 (NINETY THOUSAND!) oil wells in McKean County
alone. This is the kind of staggering statistic memorialized at the
Penn-Brad Historical Oil Well Park.

sylvania crude is paraffin-based. This makes it waxier than other crude oil, a difference you can see. Pennsylvania crude isn't black, it's greenish amber in hue, almost the color of tea.

You can see it for yourself at the Penn-Brad Historical Oil Well and Museum located on Route 219 between Bradford and Custer City, not far from where the first oil well in the area was sunk. The 72-foot-tall wooden derrick is an exact replica of the 1890s standard rigs that dotted the surrounding countryside and mountains like trees by the hundreds. What you'll learn at the Penn-Brad Oil Well and Museum is that oil wells weren't drilled so much as pounded into the ground. The drill bit was a solid iron cylinder more than six inches in diameter and seven feet in length, weighing up to 800 pounds. Behind the drill would be a 42-foot-long cylinder called a stem, which weighed 2,800 pounds. The bit and stem would be lifted and dropped by a 4½-inch-thick "bull rope," which was lifted and lowered by a wooden beam on a pivot. The beam was moved up and down by a flywheel driven by a steam engine, and in later years by a four-cylinder internal combustion engine called a Buffalo Drilling Engine.

It's all very ingenious and Rube Goldberg–looking, but it did the job. The sharpened drill bit would drop, pulverizing the bedrock. The tiny bits were then scooped up into a hollow 30-foot-long wrought iron cylinder called a bailer. When the bailer was full, it would be lifted out of the hole by the bull rope and its contents would be inspected and discarded. The drilling was done in twelve-hour shifts by two-man crews who were paid by the foot. When the contents of the bailer revealed slurry, oil mixed with rock, they had reached the oil sand located between two layers of bedrock. The drilling would continue until the next layer of bedrock was hit, letting the drillers know exactly how deep the oil sand reached. Then it was the shooter's turn.

Shooters had the most dangerous job of all. They drove mule-drawn wagons filled with nitroglycerine and dynamite, the tools of their trade. Two gallons of nitroglycerine, enough to level a city block, would be lowered into the drill hole and

# SOME SCHOOLS
# GET SNOW DAYS

*I met an old-timer at the Penn-Brad Historical Oil
Well and Museum who told me the following story:*

Back in the early 1900s when shooters, the men who
"shot" oil wells by detonating nitroglycerine deep
underground, still carried their combustibles in mule-
drawn wagons, there were occasional accidents. An
accident was generally fatal to the shooter, his mules,
any other living creatures within a quarter mile of the
explosion. Shooters had to travel over rough ground
every day in their dynamite and nitro-filled wagons, and
Custer City was in the middle of the activity.

The old-timer attended the white-clapboard one-room
schoolhouse in Custer City, and at least twice a year the
windows of the school would be blown out by the
concussion of a shooter's wagon blowing up. When the
windows blew out, school was dismissed, but not only
because of the drafty conditions. The schoolchildren then
became members of a search party looking for any
remains of the shooter, which could be scattered for
miles. The children would find bloody bits of clothing
hanging from trees and chunks of flesh (some human,
some mule) lying on the ground. The children would
gather these pieces, which would be buried, man and
animal, in the same coffin.

James Bryner, the founder of the Penn-Brad Oil Well
and Museum, told me that he'd never heard that story.
"We've got more than a hundred elderly volunteers who
work here from time to time," he said, "and some of them
are prone to exaggeration." There were shooter accidents,
that's for sure. Bryner said that as recently as 1968 a
shooter's truck exploded on the side of the road, leaving
a crater in the highway 20 feet wide and 5 feet deep.

then dynamite would be packed on top of that. The dynamite and nitro would be detonated by a heavy iron weight called a go devil that would be dropped down the well hole. Needless to say, go devils were good for one time only. The explosion 1,600 feet under the ground would create a porous crater maybe six feet in diameter, and into this crater would seep crude oil being squeezed from the surrounding oil sand by millions of tons of pressure. A pumping jack would be installed at the top of the well and crude oil would begin to flow.

Oil wells are now drilled by portable rotary drills, six or seven of which are still in operation by independent contractors in McKean County. Since 1871, a total of 90,000 oil wells have been drilled in the Bradford Oil District. The Penn-Brad Historical Oil Well and Museum is open from Memorial Day to Labor Day or by appointment. Call (814) 368–5574.

## *D - I - V - O - R - C - E* SPELLS CAMERON COUNTY
### *Emporium*

f you look at the *Pennsylvania Statistical Abstract* (and I recommend that you do, it's *fascinating* reading), you'll find Pennsylvania broken down by numbers. For instance, 6.2 Pennsylvanians people per thousand get married each year, and 3.3 per thousand get divorced (usually not the same people). Some counties' divorce rates are lower than the state average. Delaware County, for instance, has a divorce rate of 1.5 per thousand, the lowest in the state. Philadelphia is second lowest, with a divorce rate of 2.1.

Most counties fall into the mid-twos, with only Greene and Wyoming Counties cracking the fours, with divorce rates of 4.2 and 4.3, respectively. Then we come to tiny (by population)

Cameron County in North Central Pennsylvania. According to the state statistics for the year 1995, the most recent available, Cameron County has a divorce rate of 874 people per thousand.

That's not a typo. Cameron County is the "Divorce Capital of Pennsylvania" and business is booming. "We're a lot higher than we were then," said Cameron County Prothonotary David J. Reed, referring to the 1995 divorce statistics. "We handled more than 8,000 divorces in the year 2000." That would be 8,000 divorces in a county with a population of 5,800, that's a divorce rate of more than 1,600 per thousand! That's a heap of marital discord.

The divorce business is so brisk that when you call the prothonotary's office (that's where divorce papers must be filed) at the county courthouse in Emporium, the recording gives you a menu of seven choices, the first two of which are divorce related.

This has nothing to do with the rocky state of matrimony in Cameron County. It's because what Elkton is to Maryland, what Las Vegas is to Nevada, Emporium is to Pennsylvania. Except people come to Emporium to get divorced instead of married.

Unlike Elkton or Las Vegas, couples don't actually have to come to Emporium to end their marriages. Only the paperwork is necessary.

It all started in the early 1980s after Pennsylvania adopted a no-fault divorce law. Mike Davis, a lawyer in Pittsburgh, wanted to cash in on the new opportunity by offering a "simple, uncontested" divorce in the fastest time. The problem was that the courts in Allegheny County were clogged, a petition for divorce could take weeks, even months. So the enterprising lawyer started approaching the courthouses in less populated counties to see if they would process the divorces. First Davis approached Potter County (pop. 16,717) and Potter County told him to take a hike. (Potter County calls itself God's Country. Imagine the signs: Welcome to God's Country, the Divorce Capital of Pennsylvania.) So Davis came to Emporium in neighboring Cameron County and, you might say, it was a marriage made in heaven.

Each week, hundreds of divorce petitions from all over Pennsylvania pour into the Cameron County Prothonotary's Office, where they are processed and then signed by a visiting judge from Elk County. The court filing fees are a major source of income for the county. In fact, the divorce court fee income is almost half of what Cameron County reaps in property taxes. Of course, Cameron County isn't exactly advertising the fact that it has become the "Divorce Capital" of Pennsylvania. "I'd say it's a surprise to most people around here when they hear about it," says David Brown, publisher of the *Cameron County Echo,* the weekly newspaper. "It's pretty much a well-kept secret." That's what makes reading the *Pennsylvania Statistical Abstract* so fascinating! You never know what you'll find.

## HANNIBAL LECTER, MEET MAD ANTHONY
### Erie

During my travels around Pennsylvania, I found that listening to books on tape was a good way of avoiding local radio stations, both good and bad. The trouble with listening to radio on long trips through unfamiliar territory is that the worst stations tend to have the most powerful signals. And as soon as you find a station you like, you drive out of range, or a mountain interferes so that you're alternating between two stations, both of which are lousy.

I've listened to all kinds of books on tape—novels, histories, biographies—but during my trip to Erie I happened to be listening to Thomas Harris's sequel to *Silence of the Lambs. Hannibal* turned out to be the perfect companion on a stop at the Erie Historical Museum, where I found a kettle that had been used to boil the meat off the bones of Revolutionary War hero "Mad Anthony" Wayne. Wayne wasn't mad when he found himself in a stew pot on the shores of Lake Erie. In fact, he'd been

# WHERE'S LE BOEF?

*Erie takes its name from an Indian tribe that lived on the shores of the Great Lake until they were displaced by the Senecas in 1654. Erie County is the only part of Pennsylvania that shares a border with two states (New York and Ohio)and a foreign country (Canada). The French were the first white settlers and they named the nearby creek Le Boef (beef, in English) because of the large herds of bison found in the area. Even today, just south of the City of Erie, a commercial bison (beefalo?) herd can be seen to the west of I–79. The English, who won the land from the French in warfare, renamed the waterway French Creek, obviously in anticipation of a joke inspired by a TV commercial 250 years later: "Where's Le Boef?"*

dead thirteen years when his body was exhumed at the request of his son Isaac, who wanted his father's skeletal remains shipped home for burial at St. David's Church in Radnor, about 15 miles west of Philadelphia.

Well, sir, "Mad Anthony" Wayne was ornery in life and he proved to be just as uncooperative in death. Wayne died on December 15, 1796, two years after one of his greatest military victories, this time leading United States troops against hostile Indian tribes trying to stop westward expansion. The Battle of Fallen Timbers near Toledo, Ohio, in 1794 was another in a disastrous series of defeats suffered by Native Americans trying to hold on to their land. General Wayne's victory opened up the Northwest territory to Euro-American settlers. Wayne was commanding the American troops manning the garrisons in the new territory (including Fort Wayne, Indiana) at the time of his death. He was buried in a plain pine coffin in Erie, the largest town in the region.

Which brings us back to that kettle. When Wayne's body was unearthed more than a decade after his death, it was so perfectly preserved that it looked like he could have gone out to dinner that night. Because the trip to Philadelphia was almost 400 miles over rough roads, and because his son Issac had arrived to claim the body in a small sulky, there was no way to transport the entire body. So the great general's carcass was butchered. With great respect, of course. His flesh was removed from the bones and the bones were boiled white in the kettle on display in the Erie Historical Museum, next to the fava beans and a nice bottle of Chianti.

The museum, at 356 West Sixth Street, is open year-round Tuesday through Friday from 10:00 A.M. to 5:00 P.M., Saturday and Sunday from 1:00 to 5:00 P.M. Admission charged.

## *What's Up with Erie?*
### *Erie*

Pennsylvania's water boundary with Canada extends for 36 miles along Lake Erie at the northwestern tip of the commonwealth. At its greatest width, this little wedge of land reaches 16 miles north of Pennsylvania's otherwise straight-edge boundary with New York. The wedge tapers like an axe blade to the southwest until it meets the Ohio state line almost exactly where New York's southern boundary would extend. In fact, if it weren't for this little northern appendage of land that meets one of the Great Lakes, the western boundaries of the Pennsylvania would be perfectly rectangular.

Originally, five states claimed ownership of the wedge of land called the Erie Triangle, including New York, Virginia, Connecticut, and Massachusetts, all basing their claims on land grants from the king of England. Following the Revolution, the five states were persuaded to turn ownership of the land over to the new federal government of the United States, and in 1788 Pennsylvania offered to buy the land for seventy-five cents an acre. Andrew Ellicott, who would later become famous for designing the street plan for Washington, D.C., surveyed the land to be purchased and reported a total of 202,187 acres. On April 23, 1792, Pennsylvania paid the federal government $151,640.25 for the lakefront property, which may have been the best real estate deal of the eighteenth century.

### *DON'T GIVE UP THE SHIPS*
#### *Erie*

What Gettysburg was to the Civil War, what Valley Forge was to the Revolutionary War, Erie was to the War of 1812: a Pennsylvania symbol of American resolve and a turning point in war. The borough of Erie was a small lakeside town of 500 people. Its shipbuilding industry shifted into high gear when the United States declared war on Great Britain, then the greatest naval power in the world. By the summer of 1813, Erie dry docks had completed six vessels for the war effort, and on September 10, 1813, a squadron of nine American warships under the command of Commodore Oliver Hazard Perry met the mighty British in the most famous naval battle of the war fought on an inland sea. During the Battle of Lake Erie, Perry's flagship, the *Lawrence,* was brutally battered by British cannon. Eighty percent of Perry's sailors were dead or wounded when he shifted his command to the smaller *Niagara,* taking with him the *Lawrence*'s battle flag. The flag bore the dying words of Captain James Lawrence, who died in battle three months earlier: "Don't give up the ship!"

Aboard the *Niagara,* Perry quickly turned defeat into victory. Fifteen minutes after giving up his flagship, Perry forced the British commander to surrender. In his report, Perry penned words nearly as famous as Lawrence's dying command. He wrote, "We have met the enemy and they are ours."

The City of Erie never did give up the ship. Or ships. Although the *Niagara* was decommissioned and scuttled offshore in 1820, its hulk was raised in 1913 on the one-hundredth anniversary of the Battle of Lake Erie. Painstaking restoration took more than thirty years to complete, but by the 1980s the *Niagara* was beyond saving and it was finally dismantled. An exact replica was built and the new *Niagara* was launched from Erie on September 10, 1988. Today the U.S. Brig *Niagara* is one of Erie's biggest attractions, at dock or in full sail. The *Niagara* has been designated the Official Flagship of the Commonwealth of Pennsylvania; Erie is the Flagship City.

Meanwhile, a replica of the real hero ship of the epic battle, the *Lawrence,* was also reconstructed by the Pennsylvania Historical and Museum Commission and then, during a controlled experiment at a gunnery range, fired upon with cannon from the *Niagara* to replicate the actual damage caused by 24- and 32-pound cannonballs. The damaged midsection of the *Lawrence* replica is on display at the Erie Maritime Museum at 150 East Front Street. Phone (814) 452–2744.

## THESE FISH WERE MADE FOR WALKING
### *Linesville*

WELCOME TO LINESVILLE, reads the sign outside this Crawford County town near the Ohio state line, WHERE THE DUCKS WALK ON THE FISH. More than one visitor has quacked up

*You can get there from here: Downtown Linesville has a directional sign indicating that it is smack dab between New York and Chicago, a mere 500 miles either way.*

after reading that sign, but there's nothing fishy about it. Or should I say, it's very fishy? Chances are you'll see more fish in five minutes at Linesville than during a full day at the National Aquarium. The difference is that the fish at Linesville come to see people as much as people come to see them.

Just outside of town is the spillway that separates the Pymatuning Reservoir into two bodies of water, and it is along the spillway that people gather to feed the fish and the fish gather to be fed. It is, quite frankly, the darnedest thing you've ever seen. Hundreds . . . no, thousands . . . no, *gazillions* of fish swarm to the concrete edge of the spillway waiting for peo-

*Hold on tight to young children when feeding the fish at Pymatuning Reservoir near Linesville, "where the ducks walk on the fish."*

ple to toss bread into the water. The bread is devoured in a feeding frenzy by huge-mouthed carp as big as a man's forearm fighting one another for every morsel. An entire loaf of bread is gone in seconds, like a cow among piranha. It's more than a little spooky. The fish literally come out of the water and climb over each other's backs like a churning carpet of carp. Forget the ducks—a *human* could walk on the fish. Besides, all the ducks I observed remained on the edges, away from the fray.

I bought two loaves of day-old "fish bread" from the convenient souvenir concession stand next to the spillway parking lot, and everywhere I tossed the bread, the cagey carp seemed to anticipate it like a dog chasing a stick. They gathered in thick clumps six feet below the spillway railing, their mouths undulating like huge toothless *O*s getting larger then smaller then larger again. My advice: Hold your children tight when they feed the fish.

A couple of hundred yards away from the spillway is the Pymatuning Visitors Center, run by the Pennsylvania Game Commission. Inside you'll find lots of information about raccoons and deer and other wildlife, but nothing about Pymatuning's biggest tourist attraction. When I asked a uniformed Game Commission guard about the carp, he grumbled, "Ah, you'll have to ask the Department of Fish." Then he added, "They're the biggest welfare recipients in Crawford County."

He's not far from wrong. It's hard to say which came first, the people or the fish. But certainly the fish only come in large numbers because of the people bearing bread. The carp go away when the people do during the winter, and they return with the people in the spring.

The Pymatuning Reservoir was built as a public works project during the Depression. Its 17,088 acres make it the largest body of water in Pennsylvania, even though almost half of it is in Ohio. The word *Pymatuning* is of Indian origin meaning "dwelling place of the crooked-mouth man." In modern American English this might translate simply as "the White House."

## W HAT THE G ROUNDHOG S AW
### *P u n x s u t a w n e y*

G iven Pennsylvania's heavy German heritage, it is not surprising that the old-world superstitions would have made the passage with the arriving immigrants. One of those superstitions is Groundhog Day or, as it was known in Germany, Candlemas, which falls on the second of February. Perhaps "superstition" is a too strong a word to label a charming ethnic custom, but what else would you call it when humans believe that animals are invested with supernatural powers? In the case of the groundhog, the supernatural power in question is the ability to accurately predict the end of winter. As superstitions go, Groundhog Day is counterintuitive because it operates on the assumption that if the sun is shining on February 2 and the groundhog sees its shadow, then there are six more weeks of winter. If it's overcast or in the middle of a blizzard, the groundhog won't see its shadow, and therefore we can expect an early spring. Go figure.

Pennsylvania has several prognosticating groundhogs—members of the Slumbering Groundhog Lodge in Quarryville, Lancaster County, have for decades met at daybreak to divine the shadow sighting of the groundhog Orphey, the Oracle of the Octororo—but none is more famous locally or internationally that Punxsutawney Phil (known not so affectionately by the Quarryville group as "that varmint out in Punxsutawney"). Located in Jefferson County about 85 miles northeast of Pittsburgh, the borough of Punxsutawney has a population that fluctuates between 6,700 and 56,700 depending on whether or not it is Groundhog Day. Although Punxsutawney natives have been celebrating Groundhog Day officially since 1886, the event drew a modest crowd of several hundred spectators, TV cameras, and wire service reporters until 1993. That was the year Groundhog Day went Hollywood.

The charming story of a Pittsburgh TV weatherman (Bill Murray) doomed to live the same day over and over—the day being February 2, the place being Punxsutawney, Pennsylvania—became a box office blockbuster and transformed the town's previously well-known but sparsely attended Groundhog Day festivities into something of a college cult event, attracting tens of thousands to the icy tundra of western Pennsylvania in the dead of winter. "The story is just so silly, they couldn't have made it up," said Joachim Scholtz, a German immigrant, who drove to Punxsutawney from his home in Dearborn, Michigan, on February 2, 1997.

Unlike the movie, the real Groundhog Day festivities in Punxsutawney do not take place in the middle of town, but rather outside on the grounds of a rod and gun club in a small clearing known as Gobblers Knob. Here the Inner Circle, a group of top-hatted elders, confers with the groundhog named Punxsutawney Phil, "Seer of Seers, Prognosticator of Prognosticators." At 7:25 on the morning of February 2, a member of the Inner Circle pulls Punxsutawney Phil from a heated borrow inside a fake tree stump on Gobblers Knob and announces a verse whispered to him by the groundhog. If Phil saw his shadow, batten down the hatches. If he didn't, break out the T-shirts.

At least that's the theory. A computer-generated survey by the San Jose *Mercury News* in the mid-'90s reported that Punxsutawney Phil's prognostication accuracy rate over one hundred years was only 39 percent (talk about a newspaper with too much time on its hands). Accuracy aside, Punxsutawney Phil is the town's claim to fame. (This sure beats its claim to fame by the area's original inhabitants. *Punxsutawney* is from the Delaware Indian language for "dwelling place of sand flies.") The groundhog lives year-round in a heated and air-conditioned glass-enclosed lair in the Punxsutawney Library in the middle of town.

## AMERICA'S FIRST CHRISTMAS STORE
### Smethport

How America's First Christmas Store came to be in Smethport in McKean County is a story of ingenuity during the Great Depression. It was 1932 and business at Johnson's Pharmacy in downtown Smethport was slow. Proprietor Leonard Brynolf Johnson had time on his hands, so he started working on his hobby during work hours. Johnson would take pieces of wood, cut them into shapes, and them paint them as lawn ornaments. He'd make Santas and reindeer and angels and Nativity scenes and he'd leave samples of his work on display in the store. Soon customers were asking him to make them Christmas ornaments along with their prescriptions. In 1935 Doc Johnson put up his first permanent year-round Christmas ornament display, and so was born America's First Christmas Store, even though it was still called Johnson's Pharmacy until the 1950s.

As long as Johnson owned it, America's First Christmas Store had a pharmacy attached. The store expanded to take in two other storefronts and an alleyway at the intersection of Main and Mechanic Streets. The alleyway makes for a very narrow room packed with Christmas ornaments. Today the pharmacy is long gone and America's First Christmas Store is owned by Greg and Dee Buchanan. It attracts collectibles shoppers from around the world. "We've had people from South Africa and the Far East and from all over Europe," says Dee Buchanan. "Most of our business is from travelers along Route 6. During hunting season we do a lot of business with the wives of hunters while they're off hunting."

You won't find anything in America's First Christmas Store that you can't find in other stores during Christmas season,

*Inside America's First Christmas Store in Smethport,*
*the county seat of McKean County.*

but you'll find it all year round. One of the occupational haz-
ards, according to Dee, is that "the staff tends to lose the
Christmas spirit because they're surrounded by it all the time."
Imagine nonstop Christmas carols from January to July. "It
tends to become background noise," says Dee, who has become
a connoisseur of Christmas CDs. "The Beach Boys have a great
Christmas CD and so does Jimmy Buffett," she says, adding,
"But I find Elvis really depressing. 'I'll have a blue Christmas
without you'?"

Part of the cachet of buying a gift here is a tag identifying
the gift as coming from America's First Christmas Store. "We
get a lot of people who just come for the name on the tags,"
says Dee. As far as the distinction of being the first year-round
Christmas store, Dee Buchanan says, "At this point, no one has

disputed the title." Only a Scrooge would do that. America's First Christmas Store, at 101 West Main Street, is open Monday through Sunday 10:00 A.M. to 4:30 P.M. October through December. Call (814) 887–5723.

## *PENNSYLVANIA BY THE NUMBERS AND LETTERS*

P ennsylvania. Twelve letters. Four syllables (five if you pronounce the *i* and the *a* separately at the end). Four vowels (five if you count the *y*). Pennsylvania is the only state to begin with a *P* but one of twenty-one states that end with an *a*.

Pennsylvania was one of the thirteen original colonies and one of eight British colonies named in honor of a person. King Charles II of England, whose father gave his Latinized name to both the Carolinas, originally named his new colony Sylvania, Latin for woodlands. In 1681, when the lands in the New World were turned over to William Penn in payment of the 16,000 pounds sterling that King Charles owed to Penn's father, Admiral William Penn, the king added the name Penn to Sylvania.

Pennsylvania is a middling-size state in the middle of the Mid-Atlantic region. Pennsylvania ranks thirty-third in size (45,308 square miles) and sixth in population (12 million). It would take more than a dozen Pennsylvanias to fill Alaska, but it is the only state that shares a border with Canada and the Mason-Dixon line. So perfectly situated was Pennsylvania before and after the American Revolution—there were six Southern states below it and six Northern states above it—that it was called the Keystone State.

Pennsylvanians like Pennsylvania so much they rarely leave. In Pennsylvania, more people live within 50 miles of

their birthplace than in any other state. Twenty percent of
Pennsylvania's population is above the age of 60. Only Florida
has a larger proportional population of older people. Pennsylvania has more towns with populations of less than 5,000 than
any state in America. Out of 2,582 municipalities in Pennsylvania, 605—23 percent—are less than one square mile in size.
Some are so small that the Pennsylvania State Data Center lists
their total area as 0.0 square miles. The smallest are the boroughs of Shady Gap (population 113) in Huntingdon County,
Coaldale (population 143) in Bedford County, and Applewold
(population 388) in Armstrong County, all officially listed as
being 0.1 square kilometers in size.

Pennsylvania's largest city is Philadelphia (population 1.5
million), followed by Pittsburgh (population 369,879), making
Pennsylvania the only state that begins with the same letter as
its two largest cities. (Hawaii shared that distinction until its
second largest city, Hilo, was surpassed in population by
Kaliua). Philadelphia is the only city in Pennsylvania that is
also a county, covering an area of 135.1 square miles. The
entire city could fit easily inside the boundaries of two townships in sparsely populated northwestern Pennsylvania: Ship-
pen Township (population 2,495) in Cameron County is the
state's largest municipality, covering 157.2 square miles, followed by Jones Township (population 1,870) in neighboring
Elk County, which has an area of 145.4 square miles.

Pennsylvania is a commonwealth, a word derived from the
Old English term *common weal*, meaning "the public good."
Three other states—Massachusetts, Virginia, and Kentucky—
call themselves commonwealths. There is no legal distinction
between a state and a commonwealth, although commonwealth
sounds classier.

Pennsylvania is roughly rectangular in shape. Erie is
located in the northeast corner, Philadelphia is located in the
southeast corner. The distance from Erie to Philadelphia is 376
miles. The distance from Erie to Washington, D.C., is 331
miles. Go figure.

*The Kinzua Viaduct, built in 1882, was a triumph of engineering over common sense. A 2,100-foot-long wooden train trestle, 300 feet in the air? Yet today it still stands and carries tourists in steam engine trains from Kane to the far side of the valley near Mt. Jewett.*

Pennsylvania has more community names than incorporated municipalities—lots more. In the *Pennsylvania Atlas and Gazetteer* there are 4,200 communities listed between Aaronsburgh and Zullinger, roughly 1,600 more towns than municipalities. In Cameron County, for instance, there are seven municipalities (two boroughs and five townships) but twenty towns. In Fulton County there are thirteen municipalities (two boroughs and eleven townships) and twenty-nine towns. Allegheny County, on the other hand, has 130 incorporated municipalities (eighty-five boroughs, forty-one townships, and four cities) but only 110 towns. The most populous county in the state has one municipality, no boroughs, no townships, just one city, Philadelphia.

East is east and west is west, but west is best in Pennsylvania. From West Alexander to West Zollarsville, there are 136 Pennsylvania towns that begin with West, including five West Libertys, two West Bangors, two West Lebanons, and two West Mifflins. From East Allentown to East York there are ninety-four compound town names beginning with East, including two East Berlins and two East Ends. There are fifty-six towns beginning with North between North Apollo and North York, with North Washington, North Point, and North Pine Grove rating two apiece. Maybe it was a legacy of the Civil War, but there are only forty-two "South" towns, beginning with South Auburn and ending with South Williamsport. Only South Warren is duplicated, in Warren and Bradford Counties.

Pennsylvania has twenty-five Saint elsewheres, from St. Augustine to St. Thomas; St. Lawrence is named twice. There are ninety-three News, from New Albany to New Wilmington, including three New Castles, New Londons, and New Salems apiece and two New Kensingtons and two New Centervilles. There are eleven towns answering to the name Centerville. As you'd expect from a state with as many mountains as Pennsylvania, there are multiple Mounts—ninety-seven in all, from Mount Aetna to Mount Zion. And there is more duplication among Mount towns than any other compound name: 19 Mount Pleasants, nine Mount Zions, four Mount Airys, four Mount Vernons, three Mount Washingtons, three Mount Nebos, and three Mount Joys.

More Pennsylvanians claim to have German ancestry than any other national origin. Thirty-nine percent (4,316,386) of Pennsylvania residents are German, with the Irish coming in second at 20.4 percent (2,2256,143), followed by Italian (12.5 percent, 1,374,840), English (11.6 percent, 1,274,823) African (9.2 percent, 1,087,570), and Polish (8.0 percent, 882,348). Pennsylvania Dutch (143,008) account for 1.3 percent of the state population.

The Irish may have finished second in ethnic population, but no other nationality comes close to having as many Pennsylvania communities with Irish names. There are eighty-nine towns in Pennsylvania that begin with Mc, from McAdams to McWilliamstown.

# IT'S ERIE, AINT IT?

*Erie sports fans are trapped between two foreign powers—the Buffalo Bills and the Cleveland Indians—and their loyalties to Pennsylvania teams are suspect. Erie is such a foreign outpost in the minds of most Pennsylvanians that you almost expect someone from Erie to say, "How aboot a beer, eh?" like their across the lake Canadian brethren.*

*Tom Ridge is the first Pennsylvania governor to hail from Erie, and he charmed the rest of Pennsylvania with self-deprecating jokes about his hometown's relative obscurity. After he announced he was running for governor, Ridge described himself as "the guy nobody has ever heard of from the place nobody has ever been."*

# INDEX

Addley, 175
Altoona, 97–99, 99–101
Altoona Railroaders Memorial
    Museum, 99–101
America's First Christmas
    Store, 196–98
Amish, 14–16, 89, 90
Andy Worhol Museum,
    123–26
Archbald Pothole, 133–35
Ardmore, 28

Bala Cynwyd, 1
Balboa, Rocky, 33, 76, 82
Barnes Foundation, 30–31
Barnes, Dr. Albert, 30–31
Begly, Fr. Mark, 119
Bethlehem, 34
Bible, 34
Bird-in-Hand, viii
Birdsboro, 2–3
*Birdy,* 124–25
Blaisdell, George, 177–79
Bland, James, 1
*Blob, The,* 7, 8
Blue Horizon, 84–85
Body Building Hall of
    Fame, 93
Boone, Daniel, 2–3
Bradford, 173–76, 177–79
Brethren, 14–16
Bryn Mawr, 28, 150
Bryn Mawr College, 28

Buchanan, Pres. James, 26,
    27, 131
Buckingham, 3–5
Bucks County, 5–7

Calder, Alexander Milne, 57
Cameron County, 184–86
Campbell, Thomas, 148
Cannella, Francisco
    Gasparia, 18
Carlisle Indian Institute, 144
Carnegie, Andrew, 22
Carr, James "Froggy," 48–49
Centralia, 135–36
Chamberlain, Wilt, 24, 25
cheese steaks, 78–80
Chester County, 7–8
Chief Lappowinsoe, 137
Chief Teedyuscung, 56, 138
Church, Jerry, 165–67
Church on the Turnpike,
    118–20
City Hall, Philadelphia,
    66–67, 68
Clark, Dick, 61
Colwyn, 10, 11
Cornog Crossing, 18
Culp, 101–103
Curry, Charles "Chick,"
    119–20
Custer City, 180–84, 185

Daniel Boone Homestead, 2–3

Darby, 10–11
Darlington, 107
Dental Museum, 85–86
Derry Church, 21
Divorce Capital of
  Pennsylvania, 184–86
Dixon, Jeremiah, 64, 65
*Dominic and Eugene,* 124–25
Donofrio, Tony, 154–58
Douglas, Shane "The
  Franchise," 40
Douglassville, 12–14
Downington, 18
Downington Diner, 8
Drexel, Mother Katherine,
  44–47, 113
Duquesne Incline, 128–30

East Mauch Chuck, 145
Eastern Championship
  Wrestling, 39
Easton, 137–38
Edsel, 32–33
Emporium, 184–86
Ephrata Cloister, 16
Ephrata, 14–16
Erie Historical Museum,
  186–88
Erie, 186–88, 188–89, 189–90
Extreme Championship
  Wrestling (ECW), 38–40

Fairmount Park, 55–56
Fort Roberdeau, 101–103
Forty Fort, 161
French Azilum, 138–40
Friday the 13th Club, 41–42

Galeton, 163–65
Gallitzin, Fr. Demetrius,
  113–14
Germantown, 15
Gertrude of Wyoming, 148–49
Gettysburg, 59
Gibson, Josh, 126–28
Girard, Stephen, 22, 139
Glenmoore, 17–18
*Golden Slippers,* 1
Goode, Mayor Wilson, 34
Gordon, Tod, 40
Gravity Hill, 120–21
Groundhog Day, 194–95

Harley-Davidson Final
  Assembly Plant, 93–95
Harrisburg, 19–20
Heckler, Judge David, 5–7
Hershey, 20–22, 23, 24–25
Hershey Chocolate Co.,
  20–22, 23
Hickory Run State Park, 86
hoagies, 75–77
Hoffman, Bob, 91–93
Hollidaysburg, 108–109
Homan, Larry, 3–4, 124
Horseshoe Curve, 97–99

James, Betty, 108–109
James, Richard, 108–109
Jarvis, Anna, 58
Jim Thorpe, 141–43, 144–45
Johnstown, 110–11

Kane, 173
King Charles I, 26, 27

King Charles II, 26
Kinzua Viaduct, 200
Knox Mine Disaster, 20,
  151–52, 160

Lackawanna Coal Mine,
  154–58
Lancaster, 26–27
Lanza, Mario, 73–75
Latrobe, 112–13
Laurel Hill Cemetery, 57–58
Lesley, Hugh, 32–33
Liberty Bell, 69–72
Lincoln Highway, 104–106
Linesville, 190–93
Little Church, The, 17–18
Little League, 167–70
Little League Museum, *see*
  Peter J. McGovern Little
  League Museum.
Lock Haven, 165–67
Loretto, 113–14
Lower Makefield, 6

Mail Pouch Tobacco Barns,
  36–37
Main Line, 28–29
Mansfield, Jayne, 150–51
Marie Antoinette, 138–39
Mario Lanza Museum, 73–75
Mars, 115–16
Mary Meritt's Doll Museum,
  12–14
Mason, Charles, 64, 65
Mason–Dixon Line, 64–65, 200
Mauch Chunk, 145
McQueen, Steve, 7, 8

Meade, Gen. George, 58, 59
Mennonite, 14, 15
Merion, 30
Mid-City Tire, 39
Millionaires, The, 171
Mocanaqua, 146–47
Molly Maguires, 145
Moravian, 14, 15
Mr. Ed's Elephant Museum,
  105, 106
Mt. Jewett, 200
Mummers, 1, 47, 50–51
Museum of Childhood, 12–14
Mutter Museum, 60–61

Narberth, 28
National Watch and Clock
  Museum, 9
Nazareth, 34
Neumann, St. John, 44–47, 113
New Baltimore, 118–20
New Paris, 120–21
New York Knicks, 24
Nudist Volleyball Super
  Bowl, 107

Old Baldy, 59
Old Jail Museum, 141–43
Olivieri, Pat, 78
Oxford, 32–33

Paoli, 29
Pass, John, 69
Pen Argyl, 150–51
Penn, William, 14, 64, 66, 68
Penn-Brad Historical Oil Well
  Park, 181

Penn-Brad Oil Well and
Museum, 180–84
Pennsylvania Lumber
Museum, 163–65
Pennsylvania Dutch, 14
Pennsylvania Railroad, 28
Pennsylvania Turnpike, 118
Perry, Commodore Oliver
Hazard, 189–90
Peter J. McGovern Little
League Museum, 167–70
Petrich, Shirley, 10–11
Philadelphia, 14, 34–35,
38–40, 41–43, 47–51, 51–53,
55–56, 57–58, 59, 60–61,
61–63, 65, 66–67, 68,
69–72, 72–73, 73–75, 75–77,
78–80, 81, 82–84, 84–85,
85–86, 127, 128, 200
Philadelphia Art Museum, 33
Philadelphia Experiment,
51–53
*Philadelphia Inquirer,* 31, 68
Philadelphia Phillies, 38
Philadelphia Warriors, 24
Philadelphia Zoo, 53
Phoenixville, 8
Pittsburgh 122–23, 123–26,
126–28, 128–30
Port Griffith, 151–52
Potter County, 163
Pottsville, 153–54
Procrastinators Club, 41–43
Punxsutawney, 194–95
Pymatuning Reservoir,
190–93

Quarryville, 194

Remington, Frederic, 82–84
Rendell, Mayor Ed, 80
Ridge, Gov. Tom, 202
Ringling Rocks Park, 86–87
Rizzo, Mayor Frank, 34, 74
Rodin Museum, 72–73
Rolling Rock beer, 112–13
Rotheraine, L. A. "Larry,"
173–76
Ryman, Kerry, 24–25

*Saving Private Ryan,* 175
Schuylkill, 54
Schweiker, Sen. Richard, 16
Schwenkfelder, 14, 15
Scott, Dred, 26
Scranton, 154–58
Shoe Museum, 85–86
Slinky, 108–109
Slocum, Frances, 146–47
Smethport, 196–98
sneakers, 81–82
St. John the Baptist Catholic
Church, 118–20
Stallone, Sylvester, 33
Stotz, Carl, 168
Stow, John, 69

Thorpe, Jim, 144–45
Three Mile Island Nuclear
Power Station, 19–20
Three Rivers Ferry, 122
Three Rivers Stadium, 122–23
Two Street, 48

Upper Black Eddy, 86–87
USS *Eldridge,* 52–53
U.S. Brig *Niagara,* 190

Valley Forge Films, 8
Vento, Joe, 80
Villanova University, 88

Walking Purchase, 137–38
Wanamaker, John, 22
Warhol, Andy, 123–26
Warner, Glenn "Pop," 144
Warner, William, 57
Warrwick, Harley, 36–37
Wayne, "Mad Anthony,"
   186–88
Weaverton One-Room
   Schoolhouse, 89
Weightlifting Hall of Fame,
   91–93
Wellsboro, 170

West Laurel Hill Cemetery, 1
Wheatland, 27
Wheels of Soul, 62–63
White Thorn Lodge, 107
Wilkes-Barre, 160–61
Williamsport, 167–70, 171
Wister, Owen, 58
Wyoming Massacre, 146,
   148–49
Wyoming Valley, 148–49, 160

Yankee-Pennamite Wars, 146,
   160–61
Yeadon, 10
Yellow Springs, 8
York, 90–91, 91–93, 93–95
Yuengling Brewery, 153–54

Zippo Lighter Museum,
   177–79

# ABOUT THE AUTHOR

Clark DeLeon is something of a Pennsylvania curiosity himself, as friends and family members will attest. He was born in Philadelphia and always wanted to be a writer. He got his start as an editor and columnist for the daily student newspaper at Temple University. Hired out of college by the *Philadelphia Inquirer*, DeLeon wrote "The Scene" column for twenty years. His articles have appeared in numerous national publications, including *National Geographic*, *TV Guide*, *US* magazine, *Sport*, *Philadelphia*, and *Rugby* (a sport he played in his youth). DeLeon has been a reporter-columnist for NBC and CBS television affiliates and has served as a radio talk show host/commentator on local AM and FM stations. Since 1996 he has written a column for America OnLine's *Digital City Philadelphia*.